We met in the fall of 1960 when we were 17 and 14, and we became Best Friends Forever, only we didn't know then about the forever part. We dated for a year, and then we saw each other occasionally over the next four years, while we lived in different cities. Then, we lost touch with each other for the next 45 years. In 2010, 50 years after our first contact, we reconnected, reunited, and restored our bond. We realized what had always been true: the friendship we had, and still have, was and is true love. We are now married.

More than just a fairy tale come true, ours is a story of perseverance and hope – a story about the importance of never giving up, not just on love, but on life itself. Having each overcome numerous debilitating injuries and medical challenges, we now know that our future together is our reward for our perseverance and a testament to our resilience.

Our bond lasted more than 50 years. Only now do we understand and appreciate the impact that we have had on each other all that time, from our very first meeting until today. We also know now that a part of our purpose is to share our story with you. We hope that in some small way our story inspires and helps you to find your own friendship and love, your own joy and happiness, and your own perseverance and resilience.

Keep Your Smile
Never, Ever, Give Up,
Dream a Dream,
and Make It So!

Lifelong Valentines

Preface
Our Purpose in Writing

Our personal love story began in 1960 and continued through 1965, and then we lost touch with each other. We reconnected after a 45-year hiatus in late 2010. When people heard about our story, they smiled and often wanted to know more details. Of course, the story of our Reconnection also coincided with the expansion of the Internet and social media, and our love story quickly became widely known.

On February 14, 2013, an article about our love story that Art had written two days earlier, entitled "**My Lifelong Valentine**," was published on the CNN.com homepage. It was followed nine days later by publication on HuffingtonPost.com. The response was amazing, and the CNN article was viewed more than 50,000 times on the first day of its publication. The 2013 CNN "**My Lifelong Valentine**" article is reprinted in the Appendix.

At first, we were simply touched and flattered, and admittedly somewhat incredulous at all the interest. Even more surprising to us was the extent to which people repeatedly used the word "**inspiration**" in their reaction to our story. Then, as some of our recent medical challenges also became more widely known, the word "**inspiration**" was used even more frequently.

As our story began circulating more broadly on social media, we were increasingly encouraged to "write a book" or to otherwise publicize our story. Our story made people smile. Our story "**inspired**" people. But what was our story? What kind of book did we want to write? What did we want to say? What was our message? What was our purpose in writing? It has taken us seven years to answer these questions.

We knew that we did not want to write just a memoir. We were not interested in a detailed look into the rearview mirrors of our lives. It has never been in either of our natures to focus on our accomplishments, or to complain about or to seek sympathy for our challenges. Instead, we wanted to write a story that was about **hope** and **inspiration**. We wanted our story to **encourage** and **benefit** others.

Lifelong Valentines

What has become most important for us in our seven-year effort of writing this is that we both have come to recognize the extent to which our stories can, and often do, *inspire* and *influence* others. We also have a greater appreciation for the *impact* and the *hope* that our stories of overcoming our personal setbacks can provide to others.

We understand that our love story makes people *smile*. While the outlines of this story have been well known for some time, there are other aspects of our love story that we are sharing for the first time. Even we are surprised and astonished by our good luck.

Physical adversity and medical setbacks have also played a large part in both of our lives. Our challenges were never secret, but they were just not something that we discussed – at least not until social media became more popular.

There have also been other uncanny and coincidental aspects of our relationship that seem to go beyond the good luck that we both have experienced. There are clearly aspects of our story that we simply cannot explain. They just happened.

We have included pieces of Art's poetry, which really did *predict* our Reconnection and then *guide* our relationship. This was especially true during the transition time between Art's finding Barbara and Barbara's announcement two months later that we were going to get married. Poetry has made us smile. Poetry has smoothed, steadied, and anchored our lives. Poetry has helped us focus on some of the lessons we have learned over the past six decades. Poetry has helped us understand where we go from here. We hope that you will enjoy these poems now, and we hope that you will find them useful in your future.

Most importantly, we have realized that our story is not just about us. The basic elements of our story, if not the details, are about anyone who has persevered through hard times. Our story is about anyone who has bounced back from adversity. Our story is about that indomitable *human spirit* that resides within us all and that gives us all the ability to overcome the challenges that we face. Our story is about *perseverance*. Our story is about *resilience*. Our story can be about *you*. Our story is our *gift to you*.

Lifelong Valentines

A True Story That Was
Predicted and Guided by Poetry,
Made Possible by Perseverance, and
Reinforced by Resilience.

Lifelong Valentines

Our Story
An Overview

Barbara first saw Art across a Chicago high school volleyball court in the fall of 1960. She still remembers saying to herself, "*I'm going to beat him, and I'm going to meet him.*" Barbara did both. Barbara was 14, and Art was 17.

That time was magical. We dated and we were best friends, which was certainly not a common boy-girl relationship in those days. We know now that we were also in love, although we never used that word. We were young and we were shy, and besides, kids didn't talk about love in those days. Then, circumstances took over.

After our first year together, Art went to college at MIT in the Boston area in the fall of 1961, where he spent most of the next eight years. Barbara remained in the Chicago area for three more years, and then she went on to college in Madison, WI. While our friendship did continue, we drifted further and further apart as time passed. We saw each other occasionally over the next four years, but it was never the same. Oh well, we thought, it was not meant to be. We were wrong. *It was always meant to be; it was just not meant to be THEN.*

Over the next 45 years, we were increasingly aware of the impact that each of us had had on the other person, although we had no idea how great that impact really was until we reconnected in 2010. We simply lived our lives, silently touched by the memories of the other person. After our divorces, the more we each thought about it, the more we each realized how different we had been when we were together. We were not the same with others – not bad versus good, but just not as open, not as content, and not as comfortable with ourselves. We each silently wanted to be that previous version of ourselves again. Oh well, we each thought, it must just have been the innocence of youth. We were wrong. There was a truer version of ourselves, and we would ultimately find it again one day.

Lifelong Valentines

Neither of us could have known that, in our later years and long after we each had been divorced, we would each begin to search for the other. Neither of us really knew why we searched, or what we expected to find. We each just knew that we had wistful thoughts – thoughts of yearning and desire, tinged with melancholy – of the other person, of what life might have been with the other one. But, of course, these thoughts were fleeting fantasies, and we lived in the reality of the time. ***Then, suddenly one night, our reality changed. Fifty years after our first contact, Art found Barbara again. We had found our soulmates***.

~ ~ ~

We reconnected in the fall of 2010, 50 years after our first date, and 45 years after we had last seen each other. From the onset, we resumed right where we had left off: best friends able to tell each other everything. ***Nothing had changed; only time had passed***.

From the first phone call, we knew that we would spend the rest of our lives together, although it took us a little time to admit this to ourselves. Within two months, Barbara was wearing a ring. Now that we were older, it was certainly easier to talk about love than it had been when we were young. Emails, phone calls, and travel from coast to coast crowded out the rest of our lives as we filled in the details of our 45-year hiatus and dealt with plans for our future.

The transition took a year. Barbara left her friends and family, her job, and the life she had known for 30 years in La Jolla, CA outside of San Diego. She moved to Vienna VA, outside of the Washington, DC area where Art had lived for 40 years. More than a year after our Reconnection, Barbara completed the sale of her California house and the transition was officially over.

On Sunday, October 9, 2011, we were married in our living room in Virginia, accompanied by pictures of our parents, children, and grandchildren. The ceremony was performed by a judge, who had been Art's friend for many years, accompanied by his own lifelong friend and whom he would subsequently marry not long thereafter. Since we were all part of the Stargazer Band that had played at Art's house on Sunday mornings since 2002 (and which continues to this day), we had a full band session in that morning, and then changed clothes, got married, and went out to dinner with the judge and his friend.

It was, and still is, our own personal fairy tale, our own true story. It makes us smile, and it makes others smile. It inspires people. We enjoy sharing it. It is happy news in the sea of today's depressing news.

~ ~ ~

People fall in love with our love story. Many people share their own similar stories with us. Everyone likes a love story, a fairy tale that comes true. Everyone hopes for love and friendship.

As our love story has spread over the past few years, we have been told countless times that we should write a book, even make a movie. It would be so positive, so inspiring, people say. At first, we just smiled. Perhaps, we thought, but as always life is never so simple, so easy. Then, in June of 2012, our lives were profoundly changed by the latest health emergency in Art's life.

Although Art had always had routine physical exams, we were surprised to suddenly discover that he had two undetected blockages (90% and 95%) in two major arteries of his heart, as well as an irregular heartbeat. There were no definitive warning signs, but in retrospect, Art had had these conditions for years and they were about to became critical. Art's initial inclination after we took his blood pressure at home would have been "to tough it out," but fortunately Barbara took charge and called 911. Thanks to Barbara's presence in his life, as well as to the modern medical science of inserting stents into blocked arteries, Art's heart is now strong and healthy. And, while we didn't know it at the time, there would be more medical challenges to come.

Art may have been meant to find Barbara in our fairy tale,

Lifelong Valentines

But in our reality, we were both meant to take care of each other.

Both of us have experienced, and have overcome, severe health challenges throughout our lives. Both of us have come dangerously close to death. Both of us appreciate life and living in a way that can only come from facing the possibility of losing these gifts. People smile and think that it's cute that we often go to doctors and physical therapists together. People say that we both look so young and healthy for our ages (now in our 70s). We always laugh and smile knowingly.

Other details of our lives also make people smile. Barbara was in Art's poetry for over 40 years, and his poetry predicted our reunion. Art was in Barbara's deep subconscious awareness during a near-death experience in her life. These and other aspects of our lives are simply unexplainable.

When we were young, we both made a commitment to perform an act of kindness every day of our lives, and we both have honored that commitment even when we were apart. Even in high school, we each were determined to make the world a better place. As we aged, our idealistic thoughts turned into practical actions focusing on empowering people, especially women, in less-developed countries through micro loans, harnessing the power of technology for social good, helping people diagnosed with life-threatening illness, promoting open educational services, and actively supporting the arts, music, and theatre. We think alike.

Even though we were apart for many decades, both of us have lived remarkably similar lives in many respects. Both of us have realized, as we both surely subconsciously knew

*all along, that we shared similar values. We have now
come full circle.*

Our story is about what transpired beforehand that enabled us to meet and what almost prevented our Reconnection. Our story is about why we are still alive and how we survived. While our health challenges are certainly not our whole story, they have made us who we are, and they have imbued us both with compassion and with a passion for helping others.

We know that it was our positive attitudes toward life that first drew us together. We know that these attitudes have continued to invigorate our lives, both when we were apart and since we've been back together again.

It is uncanny how each of us had stayed in the recesses of the other person's mind throughout our lives. And, in retrospect, our eventual Reconnection was predictable, even though we didn't know it beforehand. It is also uncanny how medical issues played such large role in our lives, including being the key to Art's finding Barbara again.

Few people know that Barbara was severely injured in a car accident at age 19, during the period that we were dating. She was in a coma and by all odds should not have survived the accident. But she did survive. Barbara underwent numerous reconstructive surgeries and extensive rehabilitation. And Barbara not only refused to die, she thrived. Barbara beat the odds. Beautiful and athletic then and now, for example, Barbara's sorority even entered her in various beauty contests throughout the remainder of her college years, and Barbara won every time. (These were not beauty contests that Barbara, or anyone, could have chosen to enter by themselves; people had to be nominated by their organizations.) Barbara also resumed her athletic activities, which continue to this day.

Who would have predicted that Art's recovery and ability to walk again after two triple-disc back surgeries in June 2017, after a prognosis that he would never be able to walk again, would be so widely followed on social media? How would people have known about Barbara's recent challenges, including a serious bicycle accident that required stitches and hospitalization, a severe case of shingles, and the deaths of her mother and stepfather, were it not for social media? But there is more that is unpublicized. Few people know, for example, that as a result of her car accident in 1965, Barbara continues to undergo reconstructive procedures on her jaw, gums, and teeth to this day. Outwardly, there are no signs.

The Purpose
(written before November 20, 2010)

Turn around
Look back
Learn

Look ahead
Go forward
Change

Fear not
Persevere
Prevail

Turn around
Look back
Teach

Throughout our lives, both of us have found within ourselves a strength and a perseverance to prevail in very difficult and challenging situations. And, we both feel a kinship with the many others who have shared similar stories of their overcoming many kinds of adversity, in addition to their stories of finding long-lost loves.

Many people have challenges to overcome and, yes, it is not always easy to talk about one's challenges. Our story is about more than our own fairy tale come true. Our story is a message for all people who have faced challenges, whether these challenges have been overcome or not. You are not alone, and you should not be afraid to tell your story. It will inspire

Lifelong Valentines

others. You are your own fairy tale come true, and a better future is ahead of you.

Just Never, Ever, Give Up!

Lifelong Valentines

In the Beginning

Art and Barbara met on a volleyball court on a Friday night in November 1960. We owe our introduction to a dear childhood friend of Barbara's whom she had first met at summer camp several years earlier. Barbara and her friend often slept at each other's home on the weekends, since her friend lived in the city of Chicago and Barbara lived in Glencoe, IL, a suburb. Her friend's brother was a high school classmate of Art's. It was his idea that the three of them should go play volleyball at Senn High School on that Friday evening, as Barbara had been spending the weekend with her friend's family.

The volleyball games were informal. Art was the captain of one of the teams, and Barbara was a player on the opposite team. Barbara recalls:

> *Art was tall, very skinny, wore dark framed glasses, had a great smile, and walked on his toes. He was captain of the team opposite mine and he purposely picked kids for his team who obviously were not athletic. He approached the selection with kindness and compassion, not on winning*

> *the game. I admired this, and I said to myself: "**I'm going to beat him and I'm going to meet him.**"*

Lifelong Valentines

Of course, Barbara's team won, and after the game a few of us decided to go downtown to Due's Pizzeria. Due's was about six miles away from the high school and was famous for its deep-dish pizza and its long waits. In later years, deep-dish pizza became popular and its sister restaurant, Uno's, would spread throughout the nation. Barbara recalls:

> *Somehow, Art invited me to ride in his car as we all were going for pizza after the game.*
>
> *Somehow, I got to sit next to Art at a table for four. Our knees touched a lot and my young 14-year old heart went pitter patter.*
>
> *Somehow, he asked me for my telephone number, as we lived in different areas and went to different high schools.*
>
> *Somehow, he called me. I think it was on the following Sunday or Monday night. We had a fun, animated conversation. Art was very funny, and he asked me out on a date for the following weekend. I was beside myself with glee, but I was not sure how to share it with my parents because Art was a senior, lived in the city, drove a car, and was three years older than I – probably none of which would excite my parents' traditional, controlling*

> *parenting style. They had always had a closer relationship with my date, and they even usually knew my date's*

parents and family. Also, everyone I dated was my age or just a year older and had to have their parents drive us wherever we went.

Now, every time Art rereads Barbara's description of that time, he smiles and responds:

"Somehow," she says? Really? Come on! How can I not respond? Barbara was Smart. Perky. Outgoing. Determined. Friendly. Open. Cute. And on and on. What was there not to like? Barbara was then, and still is, spunky and exuberant, not timid or shy. She's still the spark plug of my life.

Barbara continues:

I cannot remember one iota about where we went on our first date, but I do remember that Art was the most fun, most interesting person with whom I had ever talked. He was very protective, very polite, and kinda' brotherly. We talked a lot about what he wanted to do for college, about how his parents did not have money and anywhere he went would have to be on scholarship. His first choice was MIT in Cambridge, MA outside of Boston – but he only could go if he got a full tuition scholarship, and then he would work odd jobs to pay for the rest.

We went to movies, but not a lot, because we didn't see each other during the week. We enjoyed our conversations and a favorite place became Walker Brothers Pancake House in Winnetka, IL. We'd share their German apple pancake – yummy! Sometimes, we would double date with friends of his who also went to Senn High School.

We dated during my freshman year at New Trier High School and Art's senior year at Senn. Sometimes, I went out with friends from my own high school, more to please my parents who were not enthusiastic about my dating Art because he was older. But no one else was as much fun or made me laugh the way Art did.

*In that first year of dating, while we were both still in high school, we also had lots of thoughtful conversations. Perhaps the most consequential of our conversations was that we both agreed to try to perform an act of kindness every day of our lives. We both kept that promise while we were apart and, of course, when we were back together again. We both practice kindness, and when asked to name our religion, we each have always said: "**Kindness**."*

~ ~ ~

As the years progressed, Art came to understand, more and more, the importance that he placed on the character traits of openness, honesty, and candor. After his divorce and after he had started to date again, whenever he would be asked by his friends what he was looking for in a woman, Art would always respond: "**openness**." **Even back then, openness is what Art liked the most about Barbara. She was a pal and pals were open with each other**.

All people, but especially teenagers, have parts of their bodies and their looks that they don't like, that make them feel embarrassed. In Art's case, one such trait was the twitching, or fasciculations, in his legs. Art was born with shortened Achilles tendons that caused him to walk on his toes. Almost from the time that he could walk, Art wore braces and special shoes, and he did exercises to correct his walk. All the early diagnoses proved incorrect, and Art's muscular, skeletal, and neurological issues have been a constant challenge throughout his entire life. The explanation, Art finally learned more than 70 years later, is that his neurological issues originated in his neck and spine, from his head to his tailbone. They were most likely the result of his being "carried wrong" in his mother's uterus.

Lifelong Valentines

By the time he was a teenager, Art had learned to ignore his constant pain and to persevere in the face of the limited capabilities resulting from his back and legs. He played all sports, and he just chose to ignore the twitching in his legs. Many years later, doctors would use sophisticated equipment to conclude the obvious: that the nerves in Art's legs were constantly firing, and that there was nothing that could be done about it. Art was not embarrassed by his skinny legs – Art was a skinny kid – but he did feel very self-conscious about his twitching legs. He avoided wearing shorts for just that reason – and then he met Barbara.

Art recalls:

> *I met Barbara on a volleyball court while I was wearing shorts, which clearly showed my twitching legs. While I had obviously worn shorts before, I had always avoided discussing my leg twitching. When I subsequently discussed this with Barbara as we began dating, it was a level of openness, honesty, and candor that I had not experienced with anyone else before then. I was astonished when she reciprocated with similar openness and honesty.*

> *To this day, I have a vivid memory of Barbara and my mother talking in our home. My mother complimented Barbara on her "cute legs and bottom," and I can still hear Barbara's reply: "I don't think that my legs or my behind are my best parts." I was stunned. I had never heard anyone, especially a girl for whom I felt an affection, talk like this.*

> *Barbara never knew that I had overheard this conversation, and she didn't recall it when we discussed it 50 years later. Yet, my admiration for Barbara was crystalized for me in that single teenage moment. I can still picture where we were standing in our home. And I still remember how much my mother also liked Barbara*

for these same reasons. Yes, Barbara was smart and cute, but it was Barbara's openness that mattered most then, and it still does to this day. I also learned 50 years later that Barbara had never cared about my twitching legs and that she felt honored that I shared this with her back then.

Barbara recalls:

I do not recall exactly why we really stopped seeing each other. What I do remember is the huge hole in my heart. I didn't think it was because Art did not like me. I did think it had something to do with my parents, their stiffness and formality towards him, and the road blocks that they had put in front of me. They hadn't ever really done that with anyone else I had dated, and I tried to excuse their stern faces when they recited the facts: Art was three years older; he drove; he lived in the city; and he was about to go away to college. Did I think they mistrusted me? No, never. Did I think it mattered to them, although not to me, that Art did not have the financial comforts that we did? Maybe.

High school years passed, quite nicely in fact. I had boyfriends; I was never without a date for a movie, a party, or a dance. I would not be truthful if I did not admit that somewhere deep inside, I missed Art. I missed our friendship, our talks, our connection, our fun. There may have been occasional letters and perhaps a few phone conversations, but it was not the same.

Then, in summer 1964 following my high school senior year, Art miraculously appeared, and I was happy. He came out of nowhere. Later, in August 1964, I had an accident with our kitchen oven that my grandfather had turned on. It was a gas oven and he did not realize it needed to be ignited by a match. The oven blew up in my face. It hurt like hell. My brother rushed me to the hospital, and I was treated for facial burns and singed hair. I looked awful. I felt worse. My parents were traveling and away. I recall waking up in my bedroom and found Art sleeping on the floor next to my bed. Art's warm, stable, comforting presence was (almost) worth the price of being burned.

At the end of August 1964, I went to the University of Wisconsin in Madison, WI, while Art returned to MIT in Boston. I was a mumble jumble of feelings. I was sad because I had just said goodbye to Art, not knowing when or if we would ever see each other again.

College began with a whirl. It was wonderful and overwhelming all at the same time. I met nice people, had a great roommate who was from Pittsburgh, made lots of new friends, was rushed by every campus sorority – I didn't realize how unusual that was at the time – and I simply enjoyed being away from home. I had lots of friends; I always had dates; and I was elected president of my sorority pledge class.

During the semester break, I went skiing with my then boyfriend and a group of friends. It was my first time and I liked it. At the end of a very good day someone cut across my skis and I went down, breaking my ankle. I was seen by the local orthopedic surgeon, given crutches (what a pain), hobbled around campus registering for classes and then at the urging of my parents decided to spend a few days at home. A friend of a friend was driving to Chicago and offered to drive me, broken ankle, crutches, and all. On the way home, we got into a snow storm and driving was hard. I had just taken off my seat belt to rearrange myself when we skidded and were hit by the car behind us – and I was the only one injured in a 5-car crash.

Lifelong Valentines

Challenges

Barbara was a passenger in a horrific car accident in January 1965, her freshman year in college. She was riding in the front passenger seat of a friend's car on a very snowy road as he drove her home from school. Barbara had just taken off her seat belt to move her then cast-covered ankle, when an elderly driver skidded into their car. Then, four more cars skidded into the wreck, pushing the first car into Barbara's side of their car. *If Barbara had had her seat belt on, she would have been killed. The movement of her body saved her life*.

Barbara went across the dashboard and through the front window. She ended up pinned behind the steering wheel on top of the driver, who survived the accident without a scratch. The rescue crew could not open Barbara's door, so they removed the driver to get to Barbara. The rescuers shouted to Barbara: "*stay awake, we will get you out*."

As luck would have it, Barbara's parent's internist was in the hospital's emergency room at the exact time that Barbara's ambulance arrived, and he said: "I know this person. Do not let the emergency room doctor operate." Instead, he insisted that two plastic surgeons, an orthopedic specialist, and a neurologist be called immediately. Then, he called Barbara's father at his office an hour away, after which he called Barbara's mother. Barbara's father beat her mother to the hospital. At some point, a nurse said: "*we're going to cut your sweater off; your mom will have to buy you a new one*."

Notified of his daughter's accident, Barbara's father raced to the hospital, jumped out of his car, left the car door open and the motor running, and barged into the operating room while the doctors were desperately trying to stabilize Barbara. He screamed to Barbara at the top of his lungs, "*Don't you die on me!*"

Deeply sedated and in a coma, Barbara still remembers hearing her father's instructions and silently vowing to do as he demanded. Barbara looked down upon herself in an out-of-body experience. and decided that the girl below was going to live. Barbara attributes her will to live throughout this ordeal to her father's command, which she remembers clearly to this day

Barbara's entire body was shattered, but her mind and spirit remained intact. She remained in a coma for ten days, and then endured many surgeries and months of rehabilitation and recovery. Her perseverance played a significant role in keeping her alive.

Years later, Barbara's mother told her that, as Barbara was eventually being moved from the recovery room into her own room, and while she was still in a coma, Barbara somehow summoned the strength and will to speak. Barbara asked her mother to tell her father that "*the accident was not Art's fault.*"

In truth, Art and Barbara had not seen each other for many months prior to the accident and we were 1,000 miles apart at the time of the accident. *Art's presence was so deeply embedded in Barbara's subconscious mind that Art was the one she thought about during that traumatic time.* Barbara did not tell Art about this story until after our Reconnection in 2010.

To ease any lingering fears that Barbara may have had, as soon as she was able to do so, Barbara's father took her for a drive past the scene of her accident. Then, even though Barbara had only been a passenger in the car during the accident, her father had her drive home.

~ ~ ~

Art's physical challenges started with his birth in 1943. Young Art could not walk like the rest of the kids. Art always knew that he was "born wrong" physically, because his parents had told him that his chin and neck had to be "straightened" at birth. Art wore back braces and special shoes from his early days though his high school years. He did special exercises. He never talked about pain or discomfort or limitations.

Despite all the gloomy prognoses that he would never be able to walk normally, let alone to play sports, Art met Barbara on a volleyball court.

Lifelong Valentines

Art was a team captain, and few people noticed that he couldn't jump quite as high as the other tall guys, that the muscles in his legs twitched, that he couldn't bend over easily, or that he couldn't even turn his head from side to side.

Barbara learned about Art's physical condition when we first met in 1960, but neither of us knew that Art was destined for two back surgeries in his early years (at ages 21 and 28) and then again for two triple-disc back surgeries (at age 74) ultimately to have rods and screws inserted in his spine. Throughout his life, doctors would tell Art that he should not have been able to walk and that he would never walk again. Art refused to accept the diagnosis then, and he is overcoming a similar diagnosis again even today. Against all odds, Art is not only walking, he's also playing drums again. As Art has always said:

> *There Is a fine line between stubbornness and*
> *perseverance,*
> *And I never know which side of the line I am on.*

If Art had not stubbornly persevered in his early years, he would not have been physically able to play volleyball on that eventful night in high school, and thus he would not have met Barbara. After his surgeries and related injuries, Art always refused to be confined to a wheelchair or to walk with crutches, although he does have a fine collection of handmade canes that have proved useful throughout his life.

Similarly, Art was only able to find Barbara many years later, because Barbara had survived breast cancer and had subsequently joined a cancer survivors' website. As a result, Art was able to learn Barbara's married name, which she had kept after her divorce 20 years previously. Barbara is now cancer free, but if Barbara had not had breast cancer, Art would not have found her.

Lifelong Valentines

And, this is the point of our telling our broader story. This is our message. This is our purpose.

Our signature photo of Art with his arm around Barbara at a fancy dinner on November 24, 1965 is our most well known and most proudly shared photo. Barbara is 19 and Art is 22. What is not well known is that this photo was taken approximately one year after both Art's first back surgery and Barbara's car accident and surgeries. Each of us had to drop out of college for a semester as a result of our surgeries and both of us took many months to recover to the point that we were able to go to this dinner. Obviously, there are no outward signs of our surgeries. And few people know of the recoveries that we were each undergoing then or the challenges that we continue to face to this day.

The larger truth is that we both have had serious medical challenges throughout our lives. We have learned that life depends upon a person's attitude. We have learned about perseverance. We have learned the true meaning of resilience. Ours is not merely a love story; ours is a life story. We not only never gave up on each other, we never gave up on ourselves. We never gave up on life.

Lifelong Valentines

Perseverance

To persevere is to overcome,
To overcome is to prevail,
To prevail is to succeed,
To succeed is to discover opportunities
That would not have existed,
If you had not persevered.

To persevere is to create opportunities
To achieve your full potential,
Because not to persevere is to fail
To live the life that you are capable of living,
And maybe even are destined to live.

To persevere is to live the life,
You are capable of living,
To live the life
You are yearning to live.

To persevere is to be the real you,
To be all that you can be,
To be the whole you.

We are pleased that people smile when they hear about our love story,
but we believe there is a deeper message in our experience. We want to
inspire you not just to find your long-lost love, but also to persevere and
to overcome your own life's challenges. We did it, and you can do it, too!

Look forward with hope

Lifelong Valentines

Waiting for Barbara

Although circumstances dictated that we lived in different cities after our first year of dating, Art never stopped thinking about Barbara. While he was in college, Art began to realize that he felt an emptiness. He harbored a longing. Not outwardly, but inwardly. He didn't try to think about it, but it was always there and occasionally it would bubble to the surface. He had liked the version of himself that he was when he was with Barbara, and he missed it. Was this just a feeling from a youthful romance, or was it more, something different, something deeper? Art was never sure.

Before and after his marriage, Art was more consciously aware of this feeling and of the different versions of himself that shared the same body. Sometimes, he was exuberant and outgoing, and sometimes, he was pensive and stoic. Sometimes, he was social and expressed his feelings, and sometimes, he was quiet and shy. One place where Art was open was in his poetry.

Art never told anyone about his poetry writing, let alone shared the poems. They were his own private expressions. Many of these poems were lost over the years, but a pattern emerges even from the ones that we have found. *Our relationship was predicted and punctuated by Art's poetry.*

In the later years preceding our Reconnection, Art did become more aware of one of the common themes and threads through his poetic writings. Art had written of an emptiness and a longing for a girl. Art did not write explicitly about Barbara, and she was never named in any of in his poems. *Art certainly did not know our Reconnection was forecast and foreordained by his poetry. Art just patiently waited and assumed that the Universe would determine when and how that time would come.*

~ ~ ~

Art's first poem, which he considers to be his signature poem, was written on the afternoon of November 22, 1963, the day that President John F. Kennedy was assassinated. President Kennedy was by then an inspirational figure in Art's life. Art was in a mathematics class in his junior

Lifelong Valentines

year at MIT when the news reached the classroom of the President's death. Art (and a few others) suggested that the class be dismissed, but the teacher refused. Art got up and left the classroom anyway.

Art went to one of the MIT libraries and wrote a poem entitled *Self-Sufficiency*. Art wrote this poem in one pass. There were no rewrites; there was no hesitancy. The poem just flowed out of him, and he can still picture himself writing it in the library.

From its writing in 1963 to our Reconnection in 2010, this poem was Art's mantra, his definition of himself. He never knew why until he and Barbara were reconnected. It was the only poem that Art had ever shared publicly, and Art would quote it frequently, especially the final part. Art was very precise about the title, and over the years he thought many times about changing the title, but he never did. It expressed what he wanted to express. Art would be self-sufficient as he went through his life. He would seek greater knowledge (education) and he would trust a greater knowledge to guide the gentle winds that blow – or, as we now know, to reconnect him with his long-lost friend, his *Lifelong Valentine*. Art would wait.

Even though Art would continue to see Barbara on occasion for at least two more years after he had written the *Self-Sufficiency* poem, Art did not share this poem with Barbara while we were still dating during those years. Art knew that being together was not meant to be, at least not then. *The issue was not an occasional meeting, but rather our being together as one, which was just not possible back then*.

Self-Sufficiency
(written November 22, 1963)

As I walk along
A bridge beneath my feet
Goals of greater knowledge
The end of life's long street

A blue expanse perceived
Serene, but oh so plain
I muse on insignificant ones
Beneath God's whole domain

Lifelong Valentines

Thoughts of a friend away so far
Understanding never to die
Words not needed to express
The feeling, I know not why

'Tis better not to question
The strange feelings that I know
But to trust a greater knowledge
To guide the gentle winds that blow

For though within us all
A spirit yearns
To be the master
Of our fate

Wise is he
Who troubles not
And alone with patience

Waits

~ ~ ~

In January 1964, two-months after writing **Self-Sufficiency**, Art sent Barbara a copy of his picture as a junior in college. On the back of the photo was a prophetic inscription that Barbara would always be the one **"by whom [Art would] gauge all others**." To his ever-lasting embarrassment, Art had misspelled the word "gauge."

Lifelong Valentines

~ ~ ~

Over the years, at least some of Art's poetry carried the same theme of an inspirational female. Sometimes, Art was more conscious of missing Barbara. Other times, he just felt an emptiness. As the years progressed, Art's feelings, themes, and melancholy were unmistakably similar, even if Art couldn't express them directly. Art had wandered in a Barbara-less desert, not knowing that someday his wandering would end. He didn't even know that he was wandering.

Our eventual **Interconnection**, our **Fusion**, was not to come for 47 more years after the writing of the **Self-Sufficiency** poem. But somehow, Art knew – or the Universe knew – or both.

Art recalls:

> *Two of my poems have always stood out in my mind. The first poem, **Self-Sufficiency**, written in **1963**, was a single-layer poem with a straightforward message. The second poem, **The Intertwining – The Fusion**, was a multilayer poem with multiple messages that only became clearer after our **Reconnection**. It is the only poem in which I have ever used words from an external source (the last verse of **Stairway to Heaven**), as well as from my own writing (the last two verses of **Self-Sufficiency**). More importantly, it*

had an interwoven message that was overlaid on the basic thoughts. The idea of our **Reconnection** was developing its own life, although I didn't realize it at the time.

This second poem was written no later than **November 6, 2007**, although possibly started earlier. This was **44 years** after the **Self-Sufficiency** poem and **three years before our Reconnection**. I recall that **2007** was also the year that I intensified my efforts to find Barbara. Then, in **2009**, **a year before our Reconnection**, I included this poem in a draft of a book that I was writing (but never finished).

Of course, I had no way of knowing in **2009**, two years after I had written this poem, that Barbara would undergo breast cancer surgery. More significantly, I had yet to learn that it was only because of Barbara's misfortune that I would finally find her another year later in **2010**.

These two poems **anticipate** and **forecast** Barbara's return. **The Intertwining – The Fusion** not only envisions our reunion, but it also envisions our spending the rest of our lives together (**our intertwining**) and our marriage (**our fusion**). Uncanny.

Even more uncanny, though, is the extent to which I wrote about, and thus called upon, the Universe to be aware of, and to take care of, Barbara. As we look back upon this three-year period, we both smile and say: "**the Universe was Aligning.**"

The Universe and I
Await the return of your exuberant soul.

BE WELL, MY EXUBERANT ONE … THE UNIVERSE AND I
AWAIT YOUR RETURN

The Universe's focus is on YOU
(Meaning: The Universe is taking care of YOU)

Lifelong Valentines

*And even more prophetic is the line in the poem that I
included twice:*

DREAM A DREAM … AND MAKE IT SO!

*I have said **"Make It So"** many times throughout my life. I
even had this statement mounted in my home office years
before I reconnected with Barbara. Was I talking to myself
in this line – or to the Universe – or to both? I don't know,
but I do know that I have always viewed these as **words to
live by**.*

~ ~ ~

The Intertwining – The Fusion
(written November 6, 2007)

STILL THINKING

And as we wind on down the road
Our shadows taller than our souls
In walks a lady we all know
Who shines white light and wants to show
How everything still turns to gold.
> *(from "Stairway to Heaven," written by Jimmy Page and
Robert Plant)*

AFTER ALL THESE YEARS

The Universe and I
Await the return of your exuberant soul.

OF YOU

For within us all a spirit yearns
To be the master of our fate
Wise is he who troubles not
> *(from "Self-Sufficiency," written by Arthur Bushkin)*

AND ALONE WITH PATIENCE

Lifelong Valentines

Waits

DARE TO BLOOM

Again

DREAM A DREAM ... AND MAKE IT SO!

There IS Peace on Earth

BE WELL, MY EXUBERANT ONE ... THE UNIVERSE AND I AWAIT YOUR RETURN

We can do no great things, only small things ...

WITHOUT YOUR GREAT LOVE,

The Universe's focus is on YOU,

WITH GREAT LOVE,

You and I

THE INTERTWINING ... THE FUSION

The Future is Now

DREAM A DREAM ... AND MAKE IT SO!

Art's Reconnection with Barbara had been clearly forecasted, foreordained, and foretold, at least from Art's point of view, although Art could not have articulated or explained why or how. It does explain, however, at least in Art's mind, why he had just assumed, from the moment we had reconnected, that we would spend the rest of our lives together. It had been decided. It had been foreordained. And, clearly Barbara's behavior would demonstrate that she felt the same way. It was never a question. Yes, there were details to work out. Yes, there were doubts. Yes, yes, yes ... but there was only one decision to be made. Would we, or wouldn't we, spend the rest of our lives together? We both had patiently waited for 45 years. The time to resume had come. We were now one, again.

The future had been forecasted, foreordained, and foretold.
The time to reunite had come.
We had never, ever, given up!

Lifelong Valentines

Searching

We had both started searching for each other many years before we reconnected. We both searched for each other even when we didn't know that we were searching for each other. We were always, at least subconsciously, looking for that long-lost friendship, for that feeling of who we each were when we were with the other one. We were always missing a piece of ourselves.

Yes, aspects of our lives had been physically difficult, but we had each maintained our spirit and our resolve. Art had had two back surgeries, and Barbara had been a passenger in a car accident. And, of course, there were many more challenges for each of us in the intervening years, but we each had persevered and we were both doing well. There were pains and physical limitations, but we were both still grateful for each day of our lives.

Curiously, not only are we asked about our attitudes during our challenging time, but we have often been asked how we pictured each other's smiles as we were searching for each other. It's a recurring question. We smile at the question, primarily because neither of us had really thought about it until after we started being asked it. We didn't have pictures in our mind's eyes of each other's smile, although now that Art has thought about it, he answers the question this way:

> *Some people have one smile. According to my mother at a very early age, I smile with my eyes, like my dad. Others smile with their mouths and show their teeth. Some people combine these two smiles. My memory of Barbara was that she had three smiles: eyes, mouth and teeth, and cheeks.*

Art does not know why he contacted Barbara that night in November 2010. He only knows that his feelings about Barbara had remained for 50 years. Barbara was always positive and upbeat, or at least she seemed that way. Barbara always brought out the best in people, the kindness and compassion that we all have, the optimism and hope for the future that lead to a happy life. Art had an image of the version of himself that he was when he was with Barbara, and as the years passed, he came to understand and like that version more and more. Art recalls:

> *What do I remember about Barbara? What drew me to search for her? I always answer that I liked the version of me that I was when I was with her. But I admit that there's more to the answer. What did I like, what did I recall, about her? What drew me to her, other than my own feelings and behaviors?*
>
> *Barbara meant serenity to me. I could remember how we were together, although not necessarily what we did. We were pals. I just liked being with her, and I wanted that feeling back again. Barbara embodied the positives of life to me.*
>
> *When I thought of Barbara over the years, of course I always thought of her eyes and her smile. Barbara doesn't just smile, she radiates. You not only see her smile, you feel it. When she smiles, you see more than her teeth and her uplifting cheeks, you are drawn into her eyes. Her smile sings to you and embraces you.*
>
> *When you have a conversation with Barbara, she doesn't only speak, she listens. When she asks about you, she is really interested in your answer. She makes you feel happy, important, and glad to be you.*
>
> *Yes, Barbara is fallibly human. Like everyone else, she has her joys and sorrows, her pains and pleasures. Yes, she experiences fear and anxiety, exhilaration and exuberance. But, then, there is that other quality, that distinguishing characteristic, that makes Barbara uniquely Barbara.*

Lifelong Valentines

Barbara is compassionate, and she is empathetic. She creates an environment, an atmosphere, and a feeling in you that she really likes you and is interested in you, and that she accepts you for who you are.

Am I biased? Sure. Blinded by love? No doubt. But then there are many others who feel the same way. People meet Barbara and feel like they've known her forever. Almost everyone immediately tells Barbara about themselves, about their lives. This happens so often that I routinely tease her whenever she's telling me about the latest person to share everything with her by asking: "Did you get their shoe size?" Barbara smiles, of course, but the experience is always the same. Medical personnel, service providers, retail sales people, friends, anyone who meets Barbara. Barbara draws out the better version of them, of anyone. All I did was get lucky and experience Barbara before almost everyone else, starting when I was 17 – and then, I recaptured it again, 50 years later. Yes, I'm lucky.

~ ~ ~

Having been divorced longer than Art, Barbara began actively looking for Art two decades before he found her. She was not seeking a relationship; she just wanted to know how Art was. She wanted to know what he had done, what path his life had taken. Barbara remembers:

I was not seeking Art as a lover when I started searching for him, but as a friend. Art was someone for whom I cared deeply, and I just wanted to make sure that he was OK. I knew that he would have been successful, but I wanted to know how he was doing as a person. I wanted to know that he was happy.

Art meant freedom, safety, and security to me. I had been taught as a child not to make waves, not to be noticed.

Lifelong Valentines

*Art empowered and provided me with a sense of
expansion and expression. Art encouraged me to hear and
express my own voice, then and now.*

*Even with all the advances in technology, people don't
know how to express, or to use, their own voices. Art
helped me to find my true voice … and he still does.*

Barbara had started looking for Art in the phone books in the Boston area where her younger son went to college, long before the Internet was the place to search for someone. Barbara also looked for Art in the airports that she visited. While she traveled extensively over the years, the odds of Barbara encountering Art at an airport were certainly not very great. Still, she tried. Perseverance.

Of course, Barbara had no idea what she would do if she were to encounter Art in one of those many airports, and Art loved to tease her about this in the early years after our Reconnection. "What would you have done, if you had found me?" Art often asked Barbara. "I don't know," Barbara always replied, "I would figure it out then." It became our ritual. Even when we travelled together after having reconnected, Barbara still instinctively looked around in the airport, only to break out laughing as she took Art's hand. Old habits die hard.

As online capabilities grew, Barbara began to use the Internet to search for Art. She easily found many references to Art, his career, and his policy writings and positions, but Barbara never looked at the dates of these articles. Instead, she mistakenly assumed that Art was still married, so she did not try to reach him. In fact, Art had long been divorced by the time that Barbara found him on the Internet. On the other hand, Art could not find Barbara online, because she had changed her last name.

Reconnecting
(November 20, 2010)

Art had searched the Internet for Barbara many times in the years prior to our Reconnection, but he had always used Barbara's maiden name, Steinback, in his searches. Invariably, these searches turned up nothing. Art had no way of knowing that Barbara had not used her maiden name since her marriage in 1968, and that she had subsequently kept her married name after her divorce. All of Barbara's adult life was chronicled on the Internet under Barbara's married name, Slavin, which Art did not know. Periodically, Art would search again for Barbara Steinback, who no longer existed, and the result was always the same. Nothing. No luck.

On Saturday, November 20, 2010, which was to be our **Reconnection Day**, Art had a full weekend day planned to do errands, attend a craft show, and write an article for submission the next day, Sunday. That Saturday was to be a busy day.

Art had attended this craft show for several decades, admiring the crafts and visiting with the artists, many of whom he had known and supported for years. Yet, something felt different. Art still cannot describe what was different about that day, or why, except to say that he felt disconnected. He was not focused on his tasks (which was not unusual), or on the craft show (which was unusual), even though he really enjoyed the show and the people. In the days leading up to that day, Art had not thought about Barbara at all, but on that Saturday morning his mind was elsewhere, not on the craft show and not on his overdue article.

Early in the morning, Art decided that he was not going to go to the craft show. No reason, he just didn't go. Instead, he puttered around the house, and ultimately did some errands and some shopping. Around dinnertime, Art sat down at his computer, but he did not begin to work on the article. He did not even think about the article. His mind was suddenly taken over by thoughts of Barbara, and he immediately started searching for her on the Internet. Art still doesn't know why, but he does know that he was very focused that evening on finding Barbara, more so than he had ever been before. He was consumed. Art remembers:

> *Once again, I started searching for Barbara Steinback (her last name when I knew her), and once again I found nothing. But the searches were somehow different this time. Google and I wrestled back and forth, and Google started to yield. The Google search algorithms, which can adapt and learn, started taking me down previously unexplored search paths, producing results that were somehow different from what I had found before. Still no Barbara Steinback, but I persevered.*

> *Finally, after considerable delay, Google produced an entirely new search path – a path that I have been unable to recreate or reproduce ever since. I found an electronic bulletin board (as it was called then) from a cabin at a girls' summer camp from the late 1950s. Only later did I learn from Barbara that she had lived in this cabin during many summers when she was in elementary school in her younger childhood, long before we had ever met.*

> *A woman, who as a young girl had been one of Barbara's cabinmates at the girls' summer camp, had posted asking if anyone knew how to find Barbara Steinback. My question exactly! I was astonished at finally finding a reference to Barbara Steinback after all my searching! I anxiously read further down the postings. Finally, I came upon a response posted by another woman who said that Barbara Steinback could now be found on the cancer survivor site, CaringBridge.com, under her married name, Barbara Slavin. (I would later learn that Barbara had had breast cancer surgery a year earlier. She has since fully recovered.)*

> *I stared at the screen, dumbfounded and disbelieving. I had found the key to my search. I now had the link*

Lifelong Valentines

between Barbara's maiden name and her current name (which I would later learn was the name that she had kept for professional reasons after her divorce). One search, one journey, had ended, and another was about to begin. I eagerly pressed forward. I was now more determined than ever. This was going to happen. I was going to find her. For the first time, success seemed possible.

I searched for the new name, Barbara Slavin, and found many possibilities, many choices – too many. I searched and cross-referenced. I went back and forth among the possibilities. I compared pictures. I tried different social media platforms, like Facebook and LinkedIn, different background sites, such as Classmates, and different search engines.

It took me awhile to decide upon the person most likely to be my Barbara. The name Slavin was common. The young girl I pictured in my mind's eyes was now of course much older. In some of the photos, she was wearing a hat (because, I later learned, some of her hair had fallen out as a result of her radiation treatments). And, some of the photos of the girl who was my Barbara had even been uploaded improperly and were distorted. Yet, there she was, I thought. The same beauty and sparkling eyes, my girl Barbara. I just knew that I had the right Barbara.

After hours of searching, I sent the same email several different ways to the person who I thought was my Barbara, hoping that at least one of those emails would reach her. Among the paths I tried for the emails were Facebook and a real estate brokers' website where I thought she might work. I never learned which of my many emails reached her, although I have always assumed that it was a Facebook message that reunited us. My email included a picture of an older me, just as I *now had a picture of the person that I thought was my older Barbara.*

*My message was simple. **"We dated many years ago in high school. Here's some information that only I would know, so you'll know that I'm real. I don't know your situation now, but I'd love to reconnect and learn how you are. Here's my contact information, and I hope that this makes you smile. If this is not you, I still hope that it makes you smile.**" I sent the email around 10:00 pm, Eastern Time, on Saturday, November 20, 2010, almost exactly 50 years after our first date and 45 years after our last date.*

About 15 minutes later, my phone rang from an area code that I didn't recognize, and a female voice said:

"Are you still awake?"

"Yes," he replied, "who's this?"

"Barbara."

My search was over! I had found my Barbara!

I had first met Barbara in the fall of 1960, and it was now the fall of 2010, 50 years later and 45 years after we had last seen each other. Little did I know then what was about to happen. My life and Barbara's life were about to change forever. The long hiatus was over.

To this day, I have not visited the CaringBridge.com site to read Barbara's cancer posts. I have, however, tried several times to recreate the search that led me to that girls' summer camp website, with no success. What did Google know that night? How did that happen? I still don't know.

Lifelong Valentines

~ ~ ~

Barbara was sitting at her desk at home using her computer when Art's email arrived. She had her walker by her side. Her reaction was one of complete and total shock. Barbara recalls:

> When I saw Art's email come across my screen that eventful night, my first response was simply, "What the ...?" I began to get tears in my eyes, and I looked up through the ceiling and said softly, "Thank you, God."
>
> I don't know how many times I read his email, maybe three, maybe six or seven. I kept thinking what could I write that would be clever and bright, yet warm? Another sigh, "What the ...!" Once I got over feeling like a teenager being home without a date on a Saturday night, I dialed one of the phone numbers that he had provided in his email.
>
> I wasn't nervous. It felt almost natural, like a connection with a dear old friend. And when I heard his voice on the other end, it sounded just like the voice I had remembered for the past 45 years. Easy. Fun. Communicative. Friendly. Warm.
>
> Not long into the conversation, I told him, "I think I've always loved you." I had hesitated for a few seconds, wondering whether I should say this, and then I just decided, why not, what the heck. I was in my sixties. I wasn't a kid any more. It was the first time I had ever used the word "love" with him, but it was true. At that moment, it meant love for my dear, long-lost friend. He had been my best friend, and when he no longer was in my life, I missed his presence. I missed the things we did, where we went, how we had talked, what we talked about. I had never had a relationship like the relationship we had shared, and I had always missed that.

Lifelong Valentines

Art had brought out the best in me. He had empowered me. He had given me the wings to fly. When he left, I retreated into a shell and formed some type of cocoon, protective and impenetrable, ceasing to be the spirited, free butterfly that I was when I was with him.

The next few days after the first phone call were like being 14 all over again. I was delightfully happy. I felt that after all the doors that had closed, now a very large, beautiful one had been opened. I felt almost giddy, free. Perhaps my luck had changed after all.

Certainly, I could not fully predict what life would be with Art. All I knew was that I had to give it my all. I had lost him 45 years ago. I didn't want that to happen again. Of course, I had many questions, from small ones to big ones, from the unimportant to the very important. I already knew, for example, that I still wanted to hear from him why he had stopped seeing me. Circumstances. It just wasn't possible then, for a variety of reasons. We both knew. We both understood.

And, I wondered, would this time be different, would the timing be better, would our relationship be lasting? I don't know if I could have said it to myself initially, but by the end of our first conversation, which lasted two and a half hours, I knew. This was it. We were back in each other's lives.

Nothing had changed; only time had passed.

~ ~ ~

Of course, just like Barbara's searching for Art in airports and not giving much thought to the possibility of finding him, Art had no idea what to expect and had not given any thought to the possibility that he might find Barbara. He had just searched. Art recalls:

I later learned that, a year earlier, in December 2009, Barbara had had breast cancer surgery. The surgery had gone well, but Barbara's recovery was difficult and prolonged, and she had developed a staph infection, which took four months to conquer. Barbara had never thought that she was going to die, and she knew that she had the spirit to persevere. However, the radiation treatments had caused several serious side effects, and she had decided to forego any further treatments.

Barbara was weak and exhausted after her cancer surgery, and she had also developed chronic nerve pain in her hands and feet, a condition called neuropathy. As a result, she had difficulty maintaining her balance and she fell several times. She ultimately tore her meniscus in her right knee. Three weeks before our fateful phone call, Barbara had had knee surgery. (Coincidentally, I had had the same surgery two decades earlier and knew that it was not fun. This was also one of the many physical conditions that we would later learn that we had in common over the years.)

Barbara had been sitting at her home office desk on that Saturday night, with her walker by her side, when my email arrived. She was so surprised that she almost fell off her chair. When people ask her about her first reaction to my email, she smiles and tells them that she was worried that she would fall off her chair and hurt her other knee.

She knew immediately that she would contact me, and her first thought was "how" to do so. She said that she didn't think she could be as clever in her reply email as I was in my email, so she simply decided to call me. Then, she "became a typical girl of her generation, and thought,

Lifelong Valentines

'what would he think about my being home alone on a Saturday night?'" That thought didn't last long, though, and she just decided, "What the heck?" So, she called me.

When she later told me this, I could easily picture that sparkling twinkle in her eyes, and that smiling mischievous look on her face. This was the same Barbara whom I had known, and she hadn't changed in 50 years, or at least so I had assumed! Clever, sparkling, and slightly mischievous. Frankly, I didn't think that my email was particularly clever. I simply pictured the same go-getter Barbara of her youth as I was writing it.

About 15 minutes after she received my email, Barbara dialed my number.

"Hello," I said, not recognizing the area code.

"Are you still awake?" a female voice asked.

"Yes," I replied, "who's this?"

"Barbara."

Although I didn't know it at the time, Barbara's search was also over – and she had not fallen off her chair.

My search was over. And, in our first conversation in 45 years, Barbara told me, among other things: "I think I've loved you all of my life." It was one of the few times in my life that I didn't know what to say next. It was a pleasant and humbling experience for me, and a harbinger of many more to come. And everyone needs a Barbara in their lives, someone who leaves them tongue-tied and speechless every now and then.

Now what?

Lifelong Valentines

We talked for two and a half hours on that first phone call. All we each had was a present-day voice and picture, and a 50-year old vision and memory. But we both knew what had just happened.

We traded pictures and talked constantly in the days and weeks ahead. It may have taken us some time to acknowledge it to ourselves, but our fate was sealed on that very first phone call. We both knew it in our hearts immediately.

There were many hurdles yet to be overcome, but we would be spending the rest of our lives together (although it was not clear from our initial conversation that we knew it at that time). What we had remembered from the past was real and always there. Fifty years after our first contact, we had reconnected. The vision was real. We had found each other, and we had found ourselves.

To Barbara, the missing boy whom she had sought in the airport, had now found her, when she wasn't looking.

To Art, the spirited girl of his youth was back in his life.

Nothing Had Changed
Only Time Had Passed

And, yes, if Barbara had not had breast cancer, Art would not have found her. To say that the darkest moments are just before the dawn is a trite phrase that is often repeated, but in this case, it was true.

Never, Ever, Give Up!
On Love and on Life

Lifelong Valentines

The Interlude

On Sunday morning, November 21, 2010, at 12:33 am, barely two hours after we had reconnected, Art sent Barbara a copy of the original ***Self-Sufficiency*** poem that he had written on November 22, 1963, almost exactly 47 years earlier.

We talked several times that next day like two old friends catching up, reuniting. It was not awkward; it was natural. It was not usual; it was familiar. It was our same ability to talk to each other with no barriers, no pretenses, and no fears. We had both changed, and we were both still the same.

There was no small talk, only honest talk. We talked about facts and details. We talked about feelings and experiences. We talked about the future. Yes, there would be hurdles to overcome, but there was no hesitancy. When we were not talking, we were emailing.

Restarting

On Sunday evening, November 21, 2010, at 10:50 pm, 24 hours after we had reconnected, Art sent Barbara an email that read in part:

> *In one of the "bizarre coincidences" category of life, John Kennedy was killed on November 22, 1963, a pivotal moment in my life. It was in response to Kennedy's assassination that I wrote the **Self-Sufficiency** poem that I have already sent you.*
>
> *Continuing with the unexplainable, I wrote the attached poem, **Courtship of a Maiden**, approximately 40 years ago – I think, but I'm not exactly sure. I found it again about 5 years ago. I never knew who the girl was. I was reminded of this poem today. I think that you remained in my life, and were an influence in my life, in ways that I*

didn't understand then, and that I still don't understand even today.

I'm looking forward to re-meeting you, or perhaps more accurately, to getting to know you. I'm also looking forward to learning more about me from you; I suspect that you could teach me a lot, and not just about myself. I've already learned much from you in these past 24 hours. Thank you.

I always thought that you were one of the happiest people I'd ever met, then or since; and that my going away would, in some ways, be best for you. I'm sorry. I never really understood the impact that I had on your life, and I do hope that our reconnecting provides you with some peace and contentment, some "closure." I never stopped caring for you or thinking about you; I just stopped seeing you.

As the Japanese would say: "sleep slowly."

Love, Art

Art sent Barbara a copy of the **Courtship** poem that he had written decades earlier. Although Art had written other poems in the intervening years, almost all have been lost.

Courtship of a Maiden
(written in early 1970s)

The hope in the face of the man still showed
    The stars twinkling in defiance
The blackness of the silent night, a fluffy blanket
    Cuddling the rocky bank
A salty sea breeze, cushioning the mossy rocks
    Water lapping at the shore's edge
Light from no apparent source, and endless sky

Lifelong Valentines

Fashioned the ballroom of the Lord
Birds and crickets, musical voices blending reality
With the ethereal calm
Rustling leaves, a softly swishing rhythm
Remembrance of a day gone by
On the velvet morning grass, a lone figure stood
His thoughts of her

~ ~ ~

Among the many side effects of Barbara's radiation and chemotherapy from her breast cancer surgery and treatment was damage to and deterioration of her already reconstructed teeth, gums, and jaw. As a result, she had to have many teeth replaced or repaired after her bout with breast cancer. This process of dental reconstruction was a result of Barbara's car accident in 1965. Barbara's recovery from breast cancer a decade ago is complete, but Barbara's treatment of her jaw, gums, and teeth continues to this day.

The extent of the damage to Barbara's teeth, gums, and jaw after her breast cancer therapy was so extensive that only a portion of her mouth could be treated at any one sitting. As it developed, Barbara was due to have gum surgery on Monday, November 22, 2010, so we agreed that we would not speak to each other that day. Besides the time difference, Barbara would be taking pain killers and would be groggy all day.

We talked throughout Sunday, November 21st, but not at all during the day on the following Monday the 22nd. Art went to bed in the evening around 10:00 pm. As usual, he turned off his mobile phone and his computers, so there would not be any sound coming from these devices. At 11:30 pm, Art awoke with a start even though he had heard nothing because his devices were turned off. Something was wrong. He just knew it. He went to his phone and turned it back on. There was a message from Barbara:

Lifelong Valentines

> *"I know that you're asleep, but I need you to wake up. I have an important question that I need to ask you,"* the *message said.*

Art threw some cold water on his face and called Barbara. It was about 11:40 pm, Eastern Time, or 8:40 Pacific Time. Barbara had slept much of the afternoon and was now partially awake. She was still groggy but resolved in her question.

> *"I need to know if this is real or if I am dreaming,"* she *asked Art. "Did we really reconnect?"*
>
> *"Yes, it was real,"* Art reassured her. *"We really did reconnect."*
>
> *"Good,"* said Barbara.

We were like two kids at a sleepover, or perhaps even like the girls in Barbara's summer camp cabin, except that we were not kids and we were on opposite sides of the country. We talked for four and a half hours, until sleepy Art could no longer stay awake. Of course, Barbara had been asleep much of the day, and she also had the advantage of the three-hour time difference. She was chatty, and she gradually woke up as Art struggled to stay awake. We never discussed the inconsistencies of how Barbara thought Art would have been able to hear her voicemail if he had been asleep … or even the fact that, since Barbara was calling Art's phone number, which she did not previously have, then this must have been real, and we must have reconnected. Sometimes, it's better just to let some things go.

Our Reconnection Had Been Confirmed

The period between our **Reconnection** (November 20, 2010) and our **Reunification** (January 17, 2011), which we call the **Interlude**, was understandably challenging, especially for Barbara. She had had serious medical issues, and she was still weak and recovering. She had not yet even resumed working from her office, and she now had to decide whether to leave her friends, her family, and her career behind in California and move to the Washington, DC area. Surely, Barbara had known Art 50 years ago, but she was now in her 60s. This was certainly not a minor decision.

In the days that followed our Reconnection, we talked and emailed constantly. Art also shared some other poetry that he had written before our Reconnection. He had wanted to make Barbara smile, and this turned out to be very helpful for us both. Poetry guided and stabilized us. It was a bridge beneath our feet. This pattern of poetry sharing continued throughout the Interlude, and then intermittently thereafter to this day. Barbara recalls:

> *Art's poetry provided me with encouragement and emotional comfort. It answered my long-held doubts about whether Art had actually liked me, thought about me, or even missed me, as these were the things that I had felt about him in the years in which we had been apart. The poetry filled in the blanks and closed the circle for me. Happily, Art's poetry showed me a side of him that I had not known before.*

As we look back, we realize that it is this poetry, rather than the specific details of the Interlude, that is the legacy of this period. Poetry anchored us. Poetry calmed us. It set the stage for future endeavors, conversations, and other activities that continue to this day, including this seven-year effort to tell our broader story.

Love of a Life
(written in early 1970s)

To thee I strain
Of birds and bees, and oh such things
With time gone by
For the school bell rings

A life of decades past
That no longer can be
Of that I yearn
But still to be with thee

Lifelong Valentines

The Man and the Sea
(written before November 20, 2010)

I am but a man
Yet, not unlike the infinite sea
Calm after a recent storm
Of which my parts have no memory

Fury unleashed, and energy spent
Rocks pounded by the wind
The wrath of One directed
At those who know they've sinned

Still no greater beauty follows
Then the sun's misty glow
A covenant of forgiveness
Sealed by the rainbow

The Open Door
(written before November 20, 2010)

The open door, a beckoning call
Yonder lies the mighty wall
Empty blackness pervades the room
For no voice returns from the silent tomb
The leaning post and the peaceful thought
All seen through the eye of love

In the first week of the **Interlude**, Art wrote a testament to gratitude for the coming Thanksgiving on that Thursday, which for Barbara confirmed that the search was over. More poetry followed.

Thanksgiving
(written after November 20, 2010)

Rustling leaves
A softly swishing rhythm
Remembrance of a day gone by

Lifelong Valentines

On the velvet morning grass
A lone figure stood

His thoughts of her

And he gave thanks

The Search is Over
(written after November 20, 2010)

I don't need to find the perfect person
I just need to find the person who's perfect for me

She was 50 years ago
And she still is today
So there's no need to wonder
"How can this be?"

She was
She is
And she always
Will be

The Trust
(written after November 20, 2010)

Throughout our lives
Each of us is given
Many keys and
Many responsibilities

Each key unlocks
A mystery of our soul
Finding each lock
A sacred lifelong goal

Opening each lock
And unraveling the mystery
Using the knowledge gained

Lifelong Valentines

A sacred responsibility

Accepting someone else's key
A gift of true love
A mystery of someone else's soul
Life's greatest responsibility

Thank you I must
For the gesture of your trust
Mindful I shall always be
Of my sacred responsibility
Guardian of the knowledge from your key
A symbol of my undying love for thee

The Spell
(written after November 20, 2010)

I must accept
I can no longer deny

The cutest one
Man has ever seen

Casts a spell
Then and now

She's smarter than a tack
Clever oh so much

An angel from above
But able to be goofy too

She dispenses trances
Like fairies sprinkle pixie dust

The spell they cast
Means I love her must

The Embrace
(written on November 30, 2010)

Lifelong Valentines

I hold you
> In awe

I see you
> With wonder

I hear you
> With amazement

I share you
> With the world
> For you are a joy
> To the world

I embrace you
> And bring you into me
> For I love you
> And fulfilled I'll be

The Better Me
(written on December 1, 2010)

I have met the other me
The one whose wisdom has shown
That there can be
A better me

I understand finally
What it takes to be free
Now that I have met
The better me

I am in awe of thee
I didn't know such a person could be
For you are the one
Who helps me be
The better me

How can I ever repay thee
My lifelong friend
The one who always knew
That there was
A better me

Lifelong Valentines

How can I express my gratitude to thee
For releasing and for liberating
For showing and for bringing out
The better me

With you by my side
Easy it shall be
No effort will it take
To be the better me

For you truly are
The better me

Re-Meeting
(early December 2010)

After our initial emails and phone calls, the obvious next step was for us to get together in person. What was it going to be like to meet each other again? We already knew what each other looked like, but what would we talk about when we were together, especially in those first few moments? Would it be awkward?

In early December 2010, Art flew from Dulles Airport in Northern Virginia to Denver, CO, where he was to change planes and then fly on to San Diego, CA. As Art was boarding the plane in Denver, he encountered a ruckus. A very upset young mother in a wheel chair was having a heated disagreement with several airline personnel.

The mother had two children with her, a 6-month old baby in her lap and a 2-year old standing beside her. According to the airline's "rules," the mother could hold the baby in her lap while she was wheeled onto the plane and assisted with getting into her seat. However, the 2-year old had to be "accompanied" by an adult while walking from the check-in desk to the child's airplane seat. For reasons which Art never understood, the airline personnel said that they were not allowed to escort the 2-year old child. Therefore, the mother and her two children could not get onto the airplane! Tears were flowing, and tempers were rising.

Lifelong Valentines

A crowd had gathered, but no one said anything. Art moved to the front, and once he understood the situation, he simply said "the child is with me." The mother and the child agreed, tears were wiped, and the airline personnel had no objection. Art walked the child onto the plane and helped him into his seat. As it developed, there were several in-and-out walks, because the plane had mechanical problems and ultimately a different plane had to be used to fly to San Diego.

Our plan had been for Barbara to wait with her car in the parking area and then meet Art just outside the baggage terminal. This was common practice at the San Diego Airport, and Art later learned that the young mother's husband, who was in the military, had also planned on doing the same thing. So, when Art landed and was exiting the airplane, he called Barbara and told her that he had arrived and that he would be carrying a 2-year old ... but that it was not his child ... and he would explain later!

Barbara had been prompt and was waiting in her car outside of the terminal. The first time Barbara saw Art inside the terminal he was carrying a child and escorting a young woman in a wheelchair with a baby. Art and the mother and the two children waited inside the terminal until the father arrived somewhat later. Art helped everyone into the car and only then was he able to turn around and say "hi" to Barbara, much to the pleasure of the airport police who were urging her to move her car.

Our first face-to-face conversation in 45 years was about a young mother and her children, and about the airlines and bureaucracy. But most importantly, it was about helping others and about kindness. It was about some of the same ideas that we had talked about when we were on dates as kids. Nothing had changed.

The Giggly Girl
(written on December 19, 2010)

I set out to be insightful
And certainly not to be frightful
But from the top of my head
Down past my tippy toes
Search as I might
I could not find a thought
That didn't cause me to bounce

Lifelong Valentines

And make my toes want to wiggle

I could find no wisdom
For which one would be grateful
And certainly no thoughts
That could be considered hateful
Just this silly muse
Which I ask you to excuse
While I try to calm my toes
By sleeping in my shoes

I thought of the girl
Who makes me want to giggle
She scrabbles my brain
And makes it turn
A snuggle into a sniggle
From my head to my toes
She itches my nose
And makes my toes want to wiggle

So I've given up
Fending off girls who make me giggle
And I've accepted my fate
That my toes they will wiggle
For there really was insight and wisdom
In this silly muse
And I will forever be
The boy who sleeps in his shoes

Now my advice to those
Who should meet a giggly girl
Who itches your nose
And wiggles your toes
Give up now
For you've really got nothing to lose
Just accept your fate
And prepare to sleep in your shoes
For that is the insight and wisdom
Of this silly muse

Lifelong Valentines

While we don't recall the exact date, Art also wrote the following email to Barbara sometime after he had visited her house in California in early December 2010.

I believe that I mentioned this quotation to you at your house.

I believe that I first heard this in my freshman year at college, obviously not long after we had been together in high school.

Regardless of when I first heard it, I have always associated this with you, and it has haunted me throughout my life.

I finally found the reference tonight, after searching for it for decades.

For all the sad words of tongue and pen,
The saddest are these:
"It might have been."
(John Greenleaf Whittier)

While we don't yet know the outcome, we do know that we have been given a second chance, another try, and perhaps a greater purpose.

We cannot reject this opportunity. We cannot avoid this possibility. We cannot not accept this responsibility. We cannot not try. We cannot be afraid.

We must pursue this purpose, at least until we know what it is. Then, we can truly decide for ourselves, instead of letting events decide for us.

We must hold each other's hand, and travel together on this journey.

My hand is outstretched, and I promise to watch over you along the way.

Lifelong Valentines

Come with me.

Not only did this make Barbara feel comforted and reassured, and but she recalls that it was this point at which she started looking forward to a future together. The fun fantasy was turning into a possible reality.

On the next to the last night of that eventful year, 2010, Art wrote:

The Angel
(written on December 30, 2010)

The heavens rejoice
And the planet sings
The trees wave
And the bells ring

The wind is gentle
And the flowers smile
Peace spreads
And hope abounds

The world has learned
The secret that I knew
Within our midst
Is the gift of you

The beauty of joy
And all that is true
The presence of an angel
The gift that is you

On January 2, 2011, Art wrote an email to Barbara entitled: "**Wow! The Future**."

Wow!

I just reread some of the poetry that I've sent you in the past weeks – some written now, and some from long ago.

Lifelong Valentines

Oh, my gosh!

This astonishes even me.

There's more, I know, and I shall search some more. ... but, upon rereading ...

The Future
(written on January 2, 2011)

The conclusion is clear
As you have said

I've always loved you
It now can be said

Deep in my heart
Not just in my head

The future is a mystery
It can still be said

But we have seen it
For the Universe has led

So now we proceed
To where we were meant to be

For I will always love you
Until I see

An onion grow
On a pretzel tree

Always and forever
I shall be

Totally and completely
One with thee

Lifelong Valentines

For there is no
Pretzel tree

On January 2, 2011, Art wrote in an email to Barbara:

Two Are One
(written on January 2, 2011)

They were together
Before they knew the meaning
Close friends bonded forever
Two were one

In the void
Distances didn't matter
Close friends bonded forever
Two remained one

Reunited again
Time has no meaning
Close friends bonded forever
Two are still one

Together into the future
They go hand in hand
Close friends bonded forever
Two always as one

On January 02, 2011, at 11:14 pm, Art wrote in an email to Barbara:

The New World
(written on January 2, 2011)

The world changed
The moment the phone rang
The sky smiled
And the trees sang

Sugar plum fairies
Did cartwheels in the air

Lifelong Valentines

And the unicorns
Dressed in colored ribbons
Galloped here and there

The tigers and lions
Danced and drank wine
The puppies and kittens
Cavorted and marched
All in a line

The gallant prince
And the beautiful princess
Held hands and kissed
And declared their love
Higher than the moon
And surely no less

The buglers sounded their call
Come one, come all
The world has changed
Know that one and all

The world has changed
Know that one and all

And it continued. On January 6, 2011, at 4:52 am, Art wrote in an email to Barbara:

Who Would Have Ever Known?
(written on January 6, 2011)

Happiness is deep in my heart
Because you are in my world
Love is back in my heart
Reserved especially for you

Who would have ever known
The sun could shine so brightly
Who would have ever thought
The flowers could smile so widely

Lifelong Valentines

Joy has new meaning
And the angels fly higher
My heart beats stronger
And my love is like fire

Who would have ever known
The sky could be so blue
Who would have ever known
That my world could contain you

The future is now possible
The music is now louder
The birds dance in the sky
Your eyes make mine brighter

The gentle caress of your touch
Brings joy to my world
And only one question remains:
How is this possible?

For who would have ever known?

And, of course, some of our many emails were also whimsical.

Our BIG New Adventure
(written on January 14, 2011)

To get to know the updated and upgraded versions of
ourselves
To learn cute small things
To learn wonderful BIG things
To create the most spectacular version of us that we can
envision
To fulfill the mission and purpose that the Universe had in
       mind for us when it undertook all this effort on
       our behalf
To conquer the world
To be together for all our days
To be truly IN LOVE

Lifelong Valentines

To be a little goofy, on occasion

I miss you

Later in the day, Barbara responded:

> *I find myself marveling at this all – from your first email
> (which, unfortunately, I may have deleted) to everything
> that has transpired and led to the conversations of these
> past few days – to my actual arrival on Monday – to get to
> see you on your turf, in your home, driving in your car in
> the city you have called home – and remembering all the
> while how in your father's car you simply pushed buttons
> to change the gears – and I wasn't even driving then! It
> seems like a dream state, but you are real, and this is
> happening! Who would've thunk [Barbara was being cute
> here and purposely misspelled this]! It's so wonderful to
> know I no longer must look for you in airports ... Sending
> love as I go to sleep.*

On January 16, 2011, the day before Barbara was to arrive in Washington,
DC, on what was to be our **Reunification Day**, Art wrote:

Reunion
(written on January 16, 2011)

The bodies met
And the spirits embraced
A time of joy it was
For each one's spirit
Had found its other home

The bodies then departed
For the time had come to roam
But the spirits stayed connected
For within each other's bodies
A part of each spirit remained in its other home

But all things end
And balance is always restored

Lifelong Valentines

The solitary journeys are now over
For the Universe has said
The bodies no longer must roam

Now the bodies are reunited
And the spirits never separated
Rejoice that the bodies are no longer alone
All are back together again
In one big happy home

All is again as it should be
And the Universe is again as it was
The stars are again aligned
And the sky is again a coat of warmth
To hug their happy home

Angels smile, and birds sing
Sugar plum fairies fly
And sprinkle pixie dust
For all are back together again
In one big happy home

And all rejoice

Barbara read this and thought to herself: All is as it should be … or, as the poem said:

The Universe is again as it was
The stars are again aligned

Later that night (with Barbara to arrive in Washington early the next morning), Art sent Barbara what he thought would be his final email entitled: "***Excitement! (and the Pledge).***" It read:

A Pledge of Gratitude: A Life of Devout Love
(written on January 16, 2011 11:54 pm)

We will be together the rest of our lives, a future both wonderful and wondrous.

Lifelong Valentines

We will share our joy and happiness, and our story of hope and love and fulfillment, with each other and with the rest of the world.

We will be a shining light of love and inspiration for each other, and a beacon of hope and love and fulfillment for others.

We will be an affirmation of reality, and a beacon of possibility.

We will be what we know we can be, and what we hope others will be.

We will be together the rest of our lives, a future both wonderful and wondrous.

This is our Pledge of Gratitude to the Universe.

This is our Devout Love for each other.

Of course, Art had difficulty sleeping that night, so naturally he wrote and sent more poetry to Barbara.

Without You
(written on January 17, 2011)

1:49 am

> I am not just not whole without you; I am not possible without you.
> I cannot just not soar without you; I cannot fly without you.
> My life is not just in your hands; my life is not a life without you.
> I am not ... without you.

2:09 am

Lifelong Valentines

You don't have to flee; you are safe with me.
What you don't seem to know, is how I am drawn to your glow.
What you don't seem to see, is how without you I cannot be.
All you must do is smile, and you light up my life.
You enlighten the world, and you enable me.
You ennoble all of humanity.

3:11 am

Do you know where to stand?
Beside me.

Do you know what to do?
Just be.

Finally, Art fell asleep. In a few hours, Barbara would arrive, and our fate together would be determined, although at that moment Art was not quite sure how it would all turn out.

~ ~ ~

Some years later, we also came to believe that it was this poem, **A Pledge of Gratitude: A Life of Devout Love**, that foretold our writing of this, our story, as it said:

We will share our joy and happiness, and our story of hope and love and fulfillment, with each other and with the rest of the world.

We will be a shining light of love and inspiration for each other, and a beacon of hope and love and fulfillment for others.

We will be an affirmation of reality, and a beacon of possibility.

Lifelong Valentines

We will be what we know we can be, and what we hope others will be.

We will be what we wish others to be.

The Test Drive
Living Together and Getting Engaged

From the time that we had reconnected, we both knew that we had to face one difficult question: namely, where would we live? For a variety of reasons, Art's home in the Washington, DC area was the obvious choice for "home base." For Barbara, this meant leaving her family, friends, and life in California, even though we readily agreed to keep Barbara's California house as a vacation home (which we never used and finally sold a year later). After Art's visit to Barbara's home in California on the first weekend in December 2010, Barbara had wrestled with her understandable ambivalence: she wanted to be together with Art, but she knew that she would also miss her established, comforting, and hard-won life in California.

We both agreed that, at a minimum, we had to "test drive" what it would be like to live together, at least for a few days and possibly for a few weeks. So, in mid-January 2011, Barbara flew from California to Florida for a preplanned weekend visit to celebrate her stepfather's birthday. Then, she got up very early on Monday, January 17, 2011, telling her parents that she was going to visit her son in New York. Instead, Barbara flew to Washington, DC. Only her son and her personal assistant knew her real plans. Barbara was not yet ready to share the fact of our Reconnection with her parents. This time she wanted to do it on her own without explanations to anyone else.

Barbara had already decided.

Art picked Barbara up at the airport around 9:00 am on Monday, January 17, 2011. Before she had even gotten into Art's car, **Barbara told Art she had decided that "we are going to spend the rest of our lives together."** Make no mistake about it, Barbara said this as a decision already made, not as something that we were still exploring. Art said, **"OK."**

Because Barbara was traveling with only a single suitcase, we had already discussed that Barbara would quickly run out of fresh clothes, in addition to her having packed for both the warm Florida weather and the cold mid-Atlantic weather. Art had offered to take her shopping, but as a first step, we had previously decided to go straight from the airport to the dry cleaners. We had planned to drop off some of Barbara's clothes and then pick them up later the next day, because there was a big snow storm predicted for the coming Wednesday. Before we had even gotten out of the car at the dry cleaners, **Barbara turned to Art and said she had decided that "we are going to get married."** Again, a decision, not a subject for discussion. Again, Art said, **"OK."**

Art thought to himself:

> **This was the same Barbara who had said to herself 50 years earlier:**
> **"I'm going to beat him and I'm going to meet him."**
> **Once again, Barbara took charge.**

Driving to his house from the dry cleaners, Art jokingly said that, since we had already decided that we were getting married, he should carry Barbara across the threshold, although he acknowledged that this probably wasn't such a good idea considering his back problems. So, Art said that he would just park in front of the house and take Barbara in through the front door and give her a tour. He would put the car in the garage later. Barbara replied fine, but no tour. Instead, she said, "since I'm going to live here, and since I am a realtor, I'd like just to go through the house myself and get a feel for everything. Then, you can show me around." OK. So be it. Art waited for 20 minutes before Barbara was ready for a tour.

For the next two days, we were just two old friends living together, like a married couple. By the snowy Wednesday, we were joking openly about our new status. Art showed Barbara his rings from his prior marriage (which had ended years earlier) that he had saved but no longer wore. Art said that of course Barbara could have any of the stones from these rings to use in making a new ring for herself. Art got down on his knees, asked Barbara to marry him, and offered Barbara the ring that she had said that she liked the most, at least as a placeholder. Barbara accepted and started wearing Art's old ring, with a fair amount of tape on the inside as padding. Now, the deal was officially done. *Two days after Barbara had arrived in Washington we were now officially engaged*.

On Friday, we went to a craft show where we saw two long-time friends of Art's who had previously made Art's prior rings. Of course, they loved Barbara immediately and the jeweler agreed to harvest the stones from Art's rings. But ... he also showed Barbara a new ring that he thought was particularly appropriate under the circumstances. This new ring had three golden garnets that matched Barbara's coloring. The three stones, he said, represented "past, present, and future."

Barbara fell in love with both the looks and the story of the jeweler's suggested ring immediately, and she started wearing it on the spot, even though it was way too big and needed to be resized. Barbara ultimately wore this ring for several months, along with a fair amount of tape on the inside as padding, before she agreed to surrender it for a few weeks to have it resized. Barbara still wears this ring to this day. And, Barbara also came to love the craft shows, which we still attend when we can.

Art and Barbara began playing house on Monday.
Art proposed on Wednesday.
Barbara began wearing her new, real, official
Engagement ring on Friday.
What a week!
And, it only took 50 years!

Sometimes, you're not wrong
You're just prematurely right!

Lifelong Valentines

Getting Married

Once we had decided that we were going to spend the rest of our lives together, we were engulfed by a flood of details. Houses. Personal belongings. Changing addresses. Finances. Furniture. Medical records and care. And the list went on and on. We worked on these details over the months.

Although we knew that we were going to get married at some point, we didn't focus on Barbara's possible name change while we were transferring Barbara's life to Virginia, simply because it was premature and because it didn't really matter that much to us. Ultimately, Barbara did decide to change her name a couple of years after we got married, and we're dealing with her prior name years later.

We also didn't focus on the standard legal issues of wills and trusts, durable powers of attorney, and advance directives. We had no differences of opinions on any of these issues. We just didn't prepare and execute all the paperwork far enough in advance, which in retrospect should have been the moment that we first decided to merge our lives.

One of the reasons that we were in no hurry to focus on our own marriage was that Barbara's younger son was going to be married during the summer of 2011. Great, we thought, and we certainly didn't want to take the spotlight off the young couple. We would wait until the fall to focus on our own marriage.

We came back home after Barbara's son's wedding and continued working on moving Barbara's various California registrations to Virginia. We also focused on rearranging the furniture and otherwise putting our new house in order. It was time to relax, we thought. Not so.

One summer night, we had dinner and enjoyed a concert with two friends. Wonderful – except that Art came home with what we would later learn was a severe case of food poisoning. After midnight, Art became so ill that Barbara finally called for an ambulance. Art was taken to a nearby hospital, where his condition continued to deteriorate. Then, a young doctor decided that portions of Art's internal organs needed to be removed immediately, although we never really learned why. Barbara was horrified and she protested. Yes, Art was clearly very ill, but couldn't, shouldn't, we wait a little bit longer? The doctor asked who Barbara was, and he was not satisfied when she answered that she was Art's fiancé. Did she have an advance directive? No, she replied. Well, then, he said, let's prepare for surgery!

Barbara continued to protest, and fortunately, Art's condition finally began to stabilize ... and we learned a valuable lesson. Now, we both carry copies of our advance directives in the glove compartments of our cars. Not surprisingly, we have had to make them available several times over the past few years. Doctors and hospitals pay far greater attention to these legal details than they did in the past.

Following Art's recovery, we began to focus on the legal details of our lives. At the same, Barbara put her California house on the market. We had always viewed this as a possible vacation home, since California represented 30 years of Barbara's life, friendships, career, life styles, memories, etc. As it developed, we had never once used this house after Barbara had made Virginia her home in the spring of 2011.

Art asked Barbara where she would live if something were to happen to him. Up to this point, we still had not taken any legal steps to redraft our personal wills and trusts, or to make the other legal and financial arrangements that would be necessary if something were to happen to one of us. And, of course, we recalled our lack of advance directives at the time of Art's food poisoning.

We called our lawyers to ask their advice, and they replied with a simple question: "do you plan to get married"? When we said that we did, the lawyers were quite clear: get married first, and then deal with all the various legal issues at the same time. This was simply too complicated to do twice.

Now, we suddenly had to hurry. Barbara had an offer on her house, and we needed time to arrange things before she travelled to California. On Thursday, October 6, 2011, Art contacted a Virginia judge, who was also a guitar-playing friend of Art's and asked if he could marry us. The judge said yes, he could, and he would even do so in our own home (versus our coming to his chambers). The only problem was that the judge was then

Lifelong Valentines

not in Virginia. He was attending a conference in Los Angeles. He would fly back on Saturday and come to our house and marry us on Sunday morning.

But judge, we said, we have band on Sunday morning. Okay, he said, he and his own lifelong friend (whom Art also knew and whom the judge would subsequently marry not long thereafter) would come to Sunday band first. Then, they would go home, change their clothes, come back and marry us in our home, and then we would all go out to a nearby restaurant for dinner to celebrate.

We moved quickly to get ready. Very early Friday morning, we went to the courthouse to get our marriage license. Then, we cleaned house. Bought flowers for the house. Arranged family pictures. Cleaned house again. Bought food for the band members (a tradition not related specifically to our imminent wedding) and bought more flowers for our wedding day. Cleaned the house once more. And, on Saturday, we each privately wrote our own wedding vows, not sharing them until we read them to each other the next day during our wedding ceremony.

Our Wedding Day
October 9, 2011

Morning

Lifelong Valentines

Afternoon

Barbara's Wedding Vows

50 years ago – You were my best friend who went away, yet always occupied a place in my heart.

I knew then, as I know today, you were the most special kind of human.

- *You who loved truth better than ego.*
- *You who remembered the value of things more than their price.*
- *You who tolerated my faults rather than condemning them.*
- *You who admitted your responsibilities to making our relationship work.*
- *You who admitted your feelings rather than denying they exist.*
- *You who explained your knowledge of facts rather than condemning me for what I may not know.*
- *You who never withheld your friendship.*
- *You who exhibited small gestures – opening a door, getting me to step outside, take a different route, and encouraging me to make a difference.*

Lifelong Valentines

You knew I had courage, yet I was afraid. You knew I could be better than I was, yet I could not find the way. You knew I had skills, yet I did not know how to develop them. I stumbled without you, but I survived. I worked hard, and I was successful. I became adventuresome and saw the world. I became a mother and then a grandmother. I was married, and I was divorced. I was sick and then I got well. I learned to value my private time and respect my aloneness.

Then you came back! The world opened in an entirely different way, yet it was similar. You once again, became my best friend. I learned more about me and I am growing. We are growing. We are playing, and we are working. We are together, and I feel safe, secure, valued, cared for, adored, respected, loved.

Once again, you are my friend and mentor, my partner and soon my husband. I am happy to be your wife. I am happy to be with you and walk together. Together we will think beyond our own existence, heal the world and make it a better place than how we found it. Together we will pass it on, times three.

Thank you, Art, for finding me – this is a fairy tale come true, and it just happens to be ours.

Art's Wedding Vows

To the Love of My Life:

Barbara, 50 years ago, you taught me many lessons – the significance of some of which I am still learning even today.

You taught me what it means to be Happy and to be Content.

Lifelong Valentines

You taught me what it means to have a true Friend.

You taught me what it means to truly care for another person – to truly be in Love – even though I doubt that I would have known to use the word back then.

For 50 years, I have measured every girl and every situation against the standard that you set.

For 50 years, I have tried to be the person who I was when I was with you, because you bring out the best in people.

Barbara, not only do I love you, but everyone who meets you, everyone who knows you, loves you.

Barbara, you are gracious and kind; you are thoughtful and compassionate; you are beautiful both inside and outside.

Now, 50 years later, the circle is complete, the past is prologue, and our future is ahead of us – and I look forward to sharing that future together.

As I told your stepfather, I let you slip through my fingers once, but I will not make the same mistake again.

Barbara, I promise to Love you ... to Honor you ... to Cherish you ... and to Protect you – for the rest of my life.

I am honored to be husband and wife.

After 51 years, the deal was finally done!

Lifelong Valentines

Reality
Differences and Similarities

She does not fully close the flip-top cap on the tube of toothpaste.

He uses any horizontal surface – the kitchen counter, the dining room table, any floor – to organize his stuff.

She cleans up his stuff, and then he cannot find it.

He talks too long when he explains things.

She prefers the strong toilet paper, which to him is too hard.

He prefers the soft toilet paper, which to her is too weak.

Fortunately, both of us believe that the toilet paper should come over, not under, the roll from the wall.

Both of us see the important things in the same way

She was the Founding Chair of the Foundation for Women, an international nonprofit organization focusing on microloans for women in less-developed countries.

He was an early supporter of micro loans and has personally funded 2,500 micro loans in 80 countries through Kiva.org.

Both of us are charitable

She has been active in many charitable organizations, including as a long-time board member of a local chapter of Rotary International.

He was the Founding Chair and CEO of the Stargazer Foundation, which focused on education and, after September 11, 2001, also on emergency preparedness and response.

Lifelong Valentines

Both of us are activists

She has taught elementary school, focusing on children with learning disabilities.

He has taught college, and always wanted to teach third grade.

Both of us are teachers.

We both have engaged in private personal philanthropy, the practice of making unsolicited gifts to people of all ages, from young children to older adults, whom we may or may not know, meet, or ever see again.

We both practice kindness, and when asked to name our religion, we each have always said: "Kindness." We always offer food and drinks to the service and delivery personnel, as well as to the guests, who come to our home. Delivery personnel often stop by our home for a drink, even when they don't have a delivery for us. We're honored.

Both of us believe in random acts of kindness

We love each other
Because we share the same values
Which we have strived to put into practice in our lives

We appreciate that we are enriched and ennobled by each other.

We know that we have been together in spirit all our lives, ever since we were first young and fell in love.

We are grateful that we are now physically together again.

Both of us are subdued and exuberant

Both of us have endured painful physical challenges, which we have overcome

Lifelong Valentines

Both of us have experienced emotional challenges, which have made us human

Both of us are older and wiser, but we are also still young and optimistic

We love each other
Because we are made better and stronger by each other

We love each other
Because we are each other

Lifelong Valentines

Feeling Grateful

Besides Art's poetry, we both would occasionally write to each other, usually via email and occasionally as a letter. Of course, we could and would also talk directly, but there was also something special about writing each other that we both enjoyed. Unfortunately, most of those writings were not saved, but we did find this very sweet piece that Barbara wrote to Art on Christmas Eve, December 24, 2014:

> *Here we are, sharing Christmas Eve. A dream that has come true. A fairy tale that happens to be real, about you and me. A story that brings tears of joy, smiles of hope, and perhaps a tad of envy to others. A story that you have told, and continue to re-tell, in various formats, that is uniquely your style in championing me, and, thereby, but perhaps unknowingly so, in championing yourself.*
>
> *You are the gift. The bestest of gifts ever. Up until four years ago I thought living a life without you was my reality. Never did I consider a life with you. Never did I consider what I would say if I ever found you in an airport.*

Lifelong Valentines

That's why I did no more than search the Internet, albeit clumsily. Or why I perused the Boston phone books when my son was at Harvard and I would visit. Or why I called 411 only to be told there was no listing for Bushkin, not in Boston, not in Chicago. I never thought I could do it – I mean initiate a reconnection. It wasn't part of my DNA. It wasn't part of my modus operandi, which was to react to life, not to create it – at least when it came to you. I was like that grown-up elephant, who was chained to a stake as an infant and had no idea of its power, its strength, its capability to pull out the stake and to venture out on its own to search for you.

This is why I like you, and in part, this is why I resist sometimes your talk of change. You did, and you still do, make me think of alternatives, think of possibilities, create options I never considered. You expand my view of me, and sometimes that view is not always positive. You cause me to rethink habits, behaviors, patterns of doing things just because that is the way I have done them for so long. You're teaching me there are other ways of behavior, especially when the space occupied is shared by two. I am less resistant to hanging on to what does not serve the best interests/solutions/answers for us, together.

Just thinking about these past four years – makes me smile, even makes me cringe at what you have gone through. Yet clearly, you won – but at great cost to you in more ways than money. You beat the problems with your house. You beat your heart challenges. In years past, you beat the odds on not being able to walk, or not being able to play sports. You always had the positive intention to make the lives of others less fortunate, better in some way.

In many ways, I believe we were aligned with each other long ago, and that alignment stayed within us. You were more assertive, certainly, in finding a way to bring it/us together again. You also have been exceedingly patient as I have stumbled along this path in the past four years, as

Lifelong Valentines

we rediscovered each other and developed a life together. Sometimes, I find myself simply grinning at the mere thought that we are where we are, finally. That you found me. That we each have survived health challenges.

You were, and still are, my protector. You make me feel safe. You make me feel that I can be more than I have been – or sometimes, think more of myself than I have in the past. I can stand tall. As you stand with me, I want to stand with you. I do think that I bring some spunk and spark to your life, that I do allow you to be smart and feel comfortable with that smartness. I think you, too, are falling into an easier step with me. We can laugh at ourselves and at each other.

*So, what's to come? First and foremost, I like simply thinking about what comes next. I like realizing that we have options. Where would I like to go with you? What would I like to learn? What must I learn? What would I like to accomplish for myself, for you, for others? Who do I want to be now that I am grown up? How can I be a better friend for you? How can I make this world just a bit better than when I arrived? **Can we rethink, revisit writing something together**? Or simply, encourage you to write something? How can I help create a better environment for us, a more balanced partnership, better communication, more laughter and joy? What about those singing lessons? What about keyboard lessons? In short, how to live each day with greater intention, with better priorities, with more accomplishments and shorter To-Do lists?*

Simply said, I thank you. Thank you for finding me. Thank you for saving my butt. Thank you for being so patient. Thank you for being such a good friend. Thank you for all the hours of mentoring, consulting, supporting me. Thank you for wanting to be healthier. Thank you for re-building our house. Thank you for helping me learn more about myself and learning to be truer. I am truly blessed, truly lucky, truly appreciative of this life – I have you babe.

Lifelong Valentines

In this piece, Barbara encouraged resumption of our writing project. Suffice it to say, various medical challenges had intervened previously, and additional medical challenges would intervene again. Although we would write bits and pieces, it would take us another three years before we would resume writing in earnest and to produce what you are reading today.

Rereading this still touches Art's heart.

Lifelong Valentines

More Difficult Days

We continued leading what we thought were normal lives, although admittedly home repair and renovation occupied a greater percentage of our time and energy than we would have preferred. We were also aware that Art's back condition was worsening. By the beginning of 2016, Art could not stand or walk, and he even had difficulty rolling over in bed. After a trip to the emergency room and nine days in the hospital with extensive tests, the doctors simply could not find the source of Art's back problem, so they just sent him home in a wheelchair with pain killers and wishes of good luck.

Barbara also had many physical issues and injuries over the past several decades, and in California she had been successfully seeing a variety of doctors and therapists for a range of treatments. Fortunately, in Virginia Barbara had discovered and was seeing several medical professionals who were part of an integrative medical practice (that is, different types of doctors, therapists, and other medical practitioners all working under the auspices of one organization).

Barbara took charge of Art's situation and called one of her therapists, who graciously came to our house on a Sunday afternoon. Art could not have possibly gotten into a car to go to an office. After an astonishing, but very gentle, treatment, Art was able to get off the massage table and walk very cautiously … and very briefly.

Art started seeing the same medical practitioners as Barbara and his condition began to slowly improve. Then, after a few months, Art's primary doctor suggested that Art's back problems did not stem (at least, not solely) from his lower back. Rather, Art's problems were also related to his neck. His neck? No doctor had ever said that before.

Art went to a special dentist who performed a CAT scan of his neck and jaw in the Spring of 2016. After the CAT scan, the dentist agreed. Art's back problems stemmed not only from his lower back, but also from his neck and jaw. Moreover, the dentist said, simply by wearing a specially crafted "appliance" on his teeth at night (much like what a teenager might wear to correct their smile), Art's neck vertebrae would slowly realign and improve his overall functioning. Art said that he would do whatever the dentist recommended, provided that the dentist would also examine Barbara, just in case she had any undiscovered residual effects from her car accident 50 years ago. The dentist agreed, and Barbara also had a CAT scan of her neck and jaw.

As it developed, Barbara did not have any direct effects from her car accident, but she did have effects from all the dental reconstruction work that she had undergone in the subsequent years. It took six months to realign Barbara's jaw and 18 months to realign Art's jaw.

After wearing the appliance at night, Art's neck vertebrae no longer protruded. He could also turn his head and his smile was no longer tilted. Unfortunately, this was not enough to compensate for all the problems in Art's lower back, and there were to be more back surgeries ahead in Art's future.

~ ~ ~

Barbara was riding her bike in July 2016 when she hit a fallen tree limb and was catapulted over the handle bar. Fortunately, Barbara was quickly found unconscious by a passerby, who immediately called 911. Barbara had a deep gash in her head, which was covered with blood. The emergency personnel found Barbara's identification and address in her bicycle bag and their ambulance took Barbara directly to the hospital. A larger hook and ladder truck went to our house, where they told Art what has just happened and urged him to go to the hospital very quickly. Barbara's head was being x-rayed when Art arrived in the emergency room, which was quite crowded.

Fortunately, Barbara's x-rays did not show any lasting damage. Several hours later, in the still crowded emergency room, Art was the only person available to assist the doctor as he shaved and put stiches in Barbara's head. Barbara remained in the hospital for only a few days, but she felt the effects of a concussion and her physical injuries for many months thereafter.

~ ~ ~

Lifelong Valentines

Despite undergoing various treatments for his back and neck, Barbara took Art to another hospital in June 2017 because he was again unable to walk. After being turned away from an overcrowded emergency room, Barbara took Art to a different hospital on the very next day. Another twenty-four hours later, on June 14, 2017, Art had emergency surgery on three lower discs in his back. Unfortunately, after reviewing the x-rays the following day, the surgeon's prognosis was that Art would never be able to walk again. Barbara said this was unacceptable and asked the surgeon what other options there were.

The surgeon said Art could undergo a second, much longer and more complex surgery to insert pins and screws in his lower spine. Bone also had to be shaved and more scar tissue removed. The surgeon said the odds of Art's ever walking again were still very low, and most people did not regain their functions after such a surgery, but it was the only other option available. Both Art and Barbara voted for this option. Art was operated on again by two surgeons this time for the same three discs in his lower back on June 19, 2017 only five days after the prior surgery. Lots of anesthesia, lots of drugs, lots of tissue, bone, and nerve trauma, and lots of uncertainty about the outcome!

~ ~ ~

Shortly after Art's second surgery, Barbara's mother, who lived in Chicago and was nearing her 97th birthday, went into the hospital. Her mother was near death physically, although mentally she was still alert. Art and others urged Barbara to go to Chicago to be with her mother.

On June 26th, Barbara caught a very early plane to Chicago and was able to be with her mother on what was to be her mother's last day. That night, Barbara and her brother together discontinued their mother's life support, as per their mother's wishes. She had designated in her advance directive that the two of them had to be present and in agreement. Barbara's mother passed away peacefully on the day after her 97th birthday.

Barbara stayed in Chicago for the week, attending the funeral and making various arrangements for her mother's apartment and effects. She then flew back to Washington, slept a few hours, and returned to Art's hospital, where she spent the next couple of days and nights continuously, not even going home to rest or get fresh clothes. Barbara then arranged for 24-hour/day private in-hospital care for Art, in addition to the on-staff nurses, after which she went home and slept.

Art was subsequently transferred from the hospital to a rehabilitation facility, only to be told after a few days that he was "not mobile enough" to remain at that facility. At the same time, Art's condition after the second surgery took a turn for the worse. He needed to return to the surgical hospital, because according to the rules, only the original surgeon could operate on him again, if another surgery were needed! Unfortunately, Art's original surgeon was then visiting South Africa. He was contacted and began to return to the U.S. As it developed, the surgeon also needed to give oral approval for Art's transfer back to the surgical hospital. This required a frantic call to the surgeon while he was changing planes in Dubai on his way back. Of course, Art was drugged, and Barbara managed the entire process.

Fortunately, the problem in Art's back was just a fluid buildup, which was ultimately drained by the surgeon, and no additional surgical procedure was required. Barbara continued to be Art's spokesperson and advocate after he was ultimately transferred to a second rehabilitation facility, where he also had around-the-clock private medical care in addition to the staff nurses and aides.

Slowly, Art regained his ability to roll over in bed, to sit, to stand, to use a wheelchair, and then to walk with a walker. After several weeks on various drugs for pain, Art began to wean himself off the pain medications. He began occupational and physical therapy. Ultimately, Art even practiced walking up and down the stairs in the stairwell, and then getting into and out of a car. He was determined to go home in Barbara's car, not in an ambulance. Of course, a therapist was always nearby, just in case Art fell, which he never did. Art ultimately spent a total of 110 days in the hospital (twice) and two different rehabilitation facilities before he was released to come home on September 30, 2017.

Art's progress at home – sitting, standing, using a wheelchair, walking with a walker, walking up and down the stairs, and then walking outside with and then without a cane – was widely followed on social media. Since only a very small percentage of the people who have had these surgeries ever do, in fact, walk again, Art's recovery has been called

Lifelong Valentines

"extraordinary" by various medical practitioners. Art now does walk (often with a cane), and he even plays drums. While his recovery is by no means complete, he has clearly defied the odds and the predictions. Here are a few of the many milestone photos that were posted on social media.

Lunch Date
(July 1, 2018)
Art's first time eating out again at a restaurant.
Besides being with Barbara, the food was good, too!

Holding Hands

Lifelong Valentines

(August 7, 2018)
Art walking around the garden holding hands with Barbara.
The first time in 14 months that Art had held hands with anyone,
Because it requires a different, and better, balance.
Barbara did not know what Art had planned to do until we had walked outside.
Never too old for surprises!

Perseverance and Resilience
(September 30, 2018)
One-Year Anniversary of Art's Homecoming

Lifelong Valentines

Lessons Learned

People who have become aware of various aspects of our broader story beyond our love story often ask us what we have learned from our experiences. What insights could we share? How have our experiences affected us?

Certainly, we're older, and hopefully a little bit wiser, than when we started upon this journey in 1960. But for most of the time, we didn't even know that we were on a journey. We didn't think about it. We were just growing up and living our lives as they unfolded before us. We were no different from anyone else. It's only in retrospect, when we turn around and look back, that at least some of our own lessons become clearer to us.

Like everyone, we would certainly do some things differently if we could live our lives over again. But no one can change the past, only learn from it. So, it is in this spirit of learning from the past that we have tried to accumulate some of the thoughts that we have collected along our journeys, separately and together.

Going Forward

You cannot edit the past, but you can change the future.
The time to start is now.

If you don't have a dream, you won't be able to leave your present to go to your future.

Each of us has a limited amount of time available to us.
Our greatest challenge is to decide what we are going to do with that time.
Our greatest mistake is to waste that time, because we think we will have more time than we end up having.
Will you have any regrets at the end of your time?
What are you going to do about it now?

Lifelong Valentines

Perfection is an ideal toward which one strives, but it
*   never really arrives.*
Continue to strive anyway.

Courage is quiet.
Strength is contentment.
Peace is perseverance.
Faith is fortitude.
You are powerful.

Your experiences are only your history
And they do not make you wise.
Your wisdom comes from understanding
What you have learned from your experiences.

Resolve

Find a way ... or make one.

Where you might see failure,
Others will see fortitude.
Go for it!
Where you might see frustration,
Others will see perseverance.
Never, ever, give up!

Give the gift of kindness every day.
You will enrich others and you will ennoble yourself.
And, you will never run out, because you have an infinite
supply.
And, it will make you feel good.

Do not fear the mountain
But tremble before the small hill
Mountains grab our attention
So respect them we will
Yet smallness is the true challenge
For it holds the lessons
That you will treasure

Lifelong Valentines

Don't worry; you will.
Have faith; you can.
Be prepared; it's soon.
And, why not you?
Why not now?

You cannot drive toward the future by looking in the
rearview mirror.
The future is in front of you, not behind you.
Tomorrow will be very different from today,
And it will look nothing like yesterday.

You're not a failure because you didn't succeed.
You're a success because you tried.

If you want to be right, be a pessimist
If you want to do right, be an optimist

Be kind to others

Tomorrow

Yesterday is long gone
And today is a short song
But your best songs are not yet sung
And your future has not yet come

It's time to live life again
And to take yourself off the shelf
Because to believe in tomorrow
Is to believe in yourself

The Better You

Turn around and look back
> *See*
> *Learn*
> *Appreciate*

Lifelong Valentines

Realize
Understand

Free yourself from
> *The ties of the past*
> *The ties of your habits*
> *The ties of perceptions long since outdated*

It may have been that way before, but it is not that way
now.
It was, but it no longer is.
You are free to decide, to determine, what will be.
You are free to be the better you.

The better future starts now,
And you will lead it.

Be what you want the other person to be.

Be kind whenever you can,
Be grateful whenever you can,
Be positive whenever you can,
You always can.

Ours is a love story that was surprisingly predicted and punctuated by Art's poetry. We can see and understand more of our own story now as we look back in retrospect, but we still cannot totally explain it all. We know that we have overcome obstacles of time and space, medical and physical challenges, and perhaps even some bad luck, but we cannot explain how it all happened. We are grateful for the time that we have had together, as well as the opportunity to pass our story along to you. We hope that we have helped enrich your life.

A few years ago, we composed a letter to send to a 30-year friend of Barbara's on the death of her husband, both of whom Art had come to know. Then, shortly thereafter, we sent a similar letter to Barbara's mother after the death of Barbara's stepfather of 27 years. We liked the

Lifelong Valentines

thoughts in this letter so much that we decided to write another, similar letter to ourselves. We offer this letter as our final gift to you.

Take Joy
A Letter to Ourselves
(October 25, 2016)

We have shown our endurance. We have demonstrated our courage. We have been our own source of strength. We have honored the love we have shared. We have been grateful for our presence in each other's life.

Together, we have made the climb and we have reached the pinnacle. We have earned the insights, perspectives, and visions that come with a successful journey. Ours has been a grand view, from coast to coast and throughout the world.

We have been inspirational for each other. We have seized each day and made it our own. We have made it our goal to be a model for others.

*When the time comes for one of us to leave, we have this wish for the other (to paraphrase the song "**It's Your World Now**" Written by Glen Frey and Jack Tempchin):*

> *A perfect day, the sun is sinking low*
> *As evening falls, the gentle breezes blow*
> *The time we shared went by so fast*
> *Just like a dream, we knew it couldn't last*
> *But we'd do it all again*
> *If we could, somehow*
> *But one of us must be leaving soon*
> *It's your world now*

Don't cry because it's over. Smile because it happened.
(Dr. Seuss)

Lifelong Valentines

With Everlasting Love,
Barbara and Art

As for us and our lives today, we look back at our signature photo and we see two young people who weren't quite ready back then to give up on life or love! We had hope. We persevered. We demonstrated resilience. We made it, and we know that you can, too!

OUR SMILES REMAINED
AND WE
NEVER, EVER, GAVE UP!

Lifelong Valentines

Keep Your Smile

Never, Ever, Give Up

Dream a Dream

and

Appendix

My Lifelong Valentine
Arthur Bushkin
CNN.com – February 14, 2013

CNN PRODUCER NOTE   *High school sweethearts Arthur*
and Barbara [Steinback Slavin] Bushkin, both
philanthropists in Vienna, Virginia, reconnected after more
than 40 years apart. 'It is a beautiful fairy tale that came
true,' Barbara said. She remembers looking for Art in every
airport she visited. 'He was a good person then, and I was
sure that goodness only got bigger as he grew up ... When
we did reconnect, his goodness was as large as the sun in
all its warmth and sunlight.'

This true story begins in the fall of 1960. Barbara saw me across a Chicago high school volleyball court and said to herself, "I'm going to beat him, and I'm going to meet him." She did both. We dated and were best friends, until circumstances intervened. I went off to college a thousand miles away, while she remained in high school in Chicago.

We were both young, and our age difference was no obstacle to love. I was a 17-year old high school senior; she was a 14-year old freshman at a neighboring high school. She smiled and was happy. She was bright and insightful. She inspired people. She brought out the best in me.

Yes, I was in love with this girl, to the extent that a young boy could know of such things. I was in love with her spirit, and the impact of her spirit stayed with me for my entire life. I liked the version of me that I was when I was with her, and that stayed with me, too. I didn't know it at the time, but I would always search for her spirit and for that version of me. The impact of our friendship never went away.

But it was not meant to be – at least, not then. I was accepted at MIT, and I spent most of the next 8 years living in the Boston area. Barbara graduated high school and went on to the University of Wisconsin. We dated off and on in our early years apart, and then we lost touch. Barbara was married two weeks after her college graduation.

In recent years, our divorces long behind us, each of us started searching for the other. Barbara had been living in La Jolla, California for the past 30 years, while I had been living in the Washington, DC area for 40 years.

In the fall of 2009, Barbara was diagnosed with breast cancer. The surgery was successful, and she spent the next year recuperating. Barbara also joined a cancer survivor's web site, not knowing that this would turn her bad luck into our good luck. Our miracle.

Fifty years after our first contact, in the fall of 2010, I would be able to find the link between Barbara's maiden name and her married name, which she (now long divorced) had used for more than 40 years. The lesson: Never, ever give up on your dreams. Always have hope. Some dreams do come true, and true love lasts.

Despite several previously unsuccessful attempts, I tried searching for her again on Saturday evening, November 20, 2010. This time, Google unexpectedly opened a new search path – a path that I have been unable to recreate ever since. I found a blog from a cabin at a girls' summer camp from the late 1950s. One girl (now a woman) asked if anyone knew how to find Barbara Steinback (her maiden name), and another girl responded that she could be found on the cancer survivor site under the name, Barbara Slavin. I had found the key to my search.

I searched for the new name and found many possibilities. It took me several hours to decide upon the one most likely to be my Barbara, because the name was common and some of the photos were distorted. I sent the same email several different ways to the person I thought was my Barbara, hoping one of the emails would reach her.

The message was simple. "We dated many years ago. Here's some information that only I would know, so you'll know that I'm real. I don't know your situation now, but I'd love to reconnect and learn how you are.

Lifelong Valentines

Here's my contact information, and I hope that this makes you smile. If this is not you, I still hope that it makes you smile." I sent the email around 10:00 pm.

A few minutes later, my phone rang from an area code that I didn't recognize, and a voice said: "Are you still awake?" "Yes, who's this," I replied. "Barbara."

We talked for two and a half hours. The spirited girl of my youth was back in my life. Nothing had changed; only time had passed. And, yes, if Barbara had not had breast cancer, I would not have found her. To say that the darkest moments are just before the dawn is trite, but in this case, it was true.

We traded pictures and talked constantly in the days and weeks ahead. It may have taken us some time to acknowledge it to ourselves, but our fate was sealed on that very first phone call. We would be spending the rest of our lives together. What we had remembered from the past was real and always there. Fifty years after our first contact, we had reconnected. The vision was real. We had found each other, and we had found ourselves.

By January 2011, Barbara was wearing a ring, and commuting between coasts. In the coming months, she quit her job, sold her house, and left her friends, family, and the life she had known for three decades, and moved to Northern Virginia. We were married in our living room in October 2011.

To be another person's soulmate is a gift that we share. We became soulmates that first night on the volleyball court, and we sealed the bond at the pizza restaurant afterwards. We had remained soulmates during our long hiatus. We were still soulmates when we reconnected 50 years later, and we are still soulmates today.

They say that love is in your brain, as well as in your heart, but friendship is something else. It's much deeper, and it's more lasting. Our friendship, and our love, have lasted a lifetime.

Lifelong Valentines

Never give up on love.